在消失的帝国旅行

Travels in a Vanishing Empire
China 1915 to 1918

The Journals of
James Archibald Mitchell

Edited by

John Hanson Mitchell
and
Hugh Powers Mitchell

Illustrated with Photographs
by the Author

Travels in a Vanishing Empire, China 1915 to 1918.
The Journals of James Archibald Mitchell

Published in the United States of America in 2017 by
Komatik Press
95 Jackson Street
Cambridge, Massachusetts 02140

www.komatikpress.com

Book design by Rex Passion

Maps © 2017, Komatik Press
Based on a map by Richard Edes Harrison in the David Rumsey Map Collection
List No. 1970.026
This file is licensed under the Creative Commons Attribution-Share Alike 3.0

ISBN: 978-0-9987113-0-0

Library of Congress Control Number: 2017936493

For Virginia Powers Mitchell
1907 - 1995

Shanghai Harbor, 1916

Contents

Foreward   vii
Preface   xi

An Incident at the Ferry, Shanghai   1
A Walk Along Soochow Creek toward Nanyang   3
Boats, Bridges, and Canals   8
The Paper Hunt   13
Trouble in Shanghai   16
Hong Kong to Canton   20
Views of Canton   30
Scout Trip to Kunshau   33
Soochow   38
A Night at the Theater   40
Chinese Wedding, Shanghai   43
Sightseeing in Peking   46
The Great Wall   65
To Tientsin and Chili Mountains   69
St. John's University   91
Funeral of a Rich Man   94
Explosions in the Night   97
Shops at Zou Ka Doo   99
Dr. Ling I-Sung   101
Thanksgiving Day   103
Shanghai Winter   105
A Lunar Eclipse   106
People of the Chinese Countryside   108
A Hunting Trip on the Grand Canal   115
Farmers Along the Grand Canal   135
Last Days in the East   138

Epilogue   154
End Notes   158
Glossary   166

Foreword

My father, James Archibald Mitchell, was born in 1892, the second child of a popular Episcopalian minister in the small town of Centreville on the Eastern Shore of Maryland. He was essentially a country boy. He lived in a world defined by seasons — chestnut-gathering expeditions in autumn, sailing and swimming in summer and spring, skating and hunting waterfowl in winter. It was, one would presume, a well-regulated, orderly Victorian household. His mother came from a landed, wealthy family and "Arch", as he was known, was sent off to Yeats School in Pennsylvanian and after graduation, entered Trinity College in Hartford, Connecticut. He went out to China only a few months later, in 1915.

Even in his younger years Arch was an avid diarist. While he was still in school, he started regularly recording daily events in a line-a-day diary in which he documented his experiences, and also to some extent, his aspirations and ambitions. He was small-framed, and his fellow schoolmates at college were almost obsessively athletic, so Arch was up against fierce competition and had to work hard to maintain himself on the playing fields. He was also a serious student and a deep reader, and although he does not say so in his diaries, he apparently acquitted himself well. He was a popular figure on the college campus and graduated with honors.

Given his position in his small world, one has to wonder why, with such a strong local base, he would cast off all his roots, friends, and family, and set out for the long journey to China.

Part of the answer may be found in his diary from his first year in college. On November 10th, 1911, his mother died. Then on the same day, a month later, his father died.

For a boy from a small, comfortable town in rural Maryland, facing the rigors of a cold northern, highly competitive college was hard enough. But to lose one's parents in the space of a month early in his first year at college was a devastating blow. His daily records dry up during this period.

The loss of his parents and his deepening spirituality and concomitant social concerns must have sent him into something of a dark night of the soul that was resolved by throwing off the world he had known and heading East to do what he felt was good, charitable work as a teacher at a Christian missionary college.

This was also a great adventure. He was twenty-four, in good health, and there was more to his world than the closed social life of the Eastern Shore, and so he set out.

The journals are almost a narrative of the traditional hero's quest. The voyage to China itself was something of an odyssey. It took twenty-four days to reach Shanghai, and even though there were thousands of Westerners living in the protected foreign compounds, travel in the rural areas, which he often undertook, was not entirely safe. There were opposing armies at each other's throats, and there were roving gangs of bandits in some sections of the country. The appearance of white people in the small rural villages was a source of great amazement to the locals. But Arch soldiered on. Like the traditional hero of quest literature, he entered into an alien, unknown world, an innocent abroad, traveled through the country, and came back, finally, as a new, more enlightened figure.

Arch left home for China on August 7th., 1915 and with his sister Sue, traveled by train to the West Coast, stopping along the way in Chicago and the Grand Canyon. On August 22nd., he boarded the Japanese steamer *Nipon Maru* in Santa Barbara, and after a calm and uneventful crossing, arrived at Yokohama, on September 7th.. A few days later, he boarded a local steamer and headed for Shanghai.

The journal covering his travels en route to China is a daily record typical of travel diaries of the period. It is when he lands in Yokohama that his descriptions of the colors, the sounds and smells, the people, and the exoticism of the landscapes that characterize the body of the three years of journal entries come into full flower.

The journals begin with a description of the soft footsteps of the rickshaw men as they pass to and fro on the quiet night streets of Yo-kohama. He describes the close heat, the narrow streets crowded with rickshaws, wheelbarrows, pedestrians, and donkeys, and the friendly but constant, stares of the crowds that gather to view the passage of the strange white-skinned creature so recently arrived in their midst.

A few days later, he boarded a small coastal steamer for Shanghai and on September 15th, approached the city on the Huangpu River. He was up early that day for the journey up the river and was surprised at the greenness of the banks. As Shanghai itself hove into view, he was surprised again by the modernity of the city. The Bund, the water-front of Shanghai, was characterized, even then in 1915, by Western architectural-styled buildings. There was little that was Chinese about the whole scene, a shock to him; he was expecting a more exotic en-vironment. He wrestled his trunks aboard a launch that carried the passengers to shore, landed, and worked his way through customs, and after an hour or so, stepped out into China, where he would remain for the next three years.

His first impressions of the mysterious and, to him, exotic East are fresh accounts of his pure amazement at it all. But as the weeks and months progress, the writing becomes more journalistically objective.

Perhaps the most telling entry of this acclimation to the Chinese world occurs on June 16th in 1916, a little under a year after his arrival. It is evidence both of his objectivity and of the influence that China had had on him by that time.

He was looking out of his window on a hot day of steady rain at the view beyond the compound. On the opposite bank of Sozhou Creek, there were three water buffalo comfortably chewing their cuds. One was lying down, and a lone Chinese man in a bizarre straw rain cloak and a wide hat, sat stolidly on his back. A solitary junk, its tat-tered sail lowered, was sculling by on the still waters, and downstream, among the junks tied to the opposite banks, a man was washing his bowl of rice. On the other side of the creek the open fields of green crops stretched away, broken only by the many conical grave mounds, with occasional paths winding through the scene.

For some reason, Arch was reminded of a similarly rainy day in New York City, as he watched the hurrying crowds of theatergoers pass by on Broadway. The contrast was striking — that there could be two such antithetical scenes in the world, and yet it was New York that seemed unreal.

That was after a year in China, by which time he was approaching the status of "Old China Hand", as so many who spent years in the East were known after their return. He was fluent enough in the Shanghaiese to make himself understood in his local travels and, while traveling farther afield, he was even able to get by in Mandarin. And although he was homesick in his first few weeks, he was soon swept into the color and excitement of the new world he had joined.

John Hanson Mitchell, Littleton, Massachusetts, 2017

Preface

前言

There were armies clashing throughout China in those desperate years. The ancient Manchu Qing Dynasty had fallen, the Empress Dowager, Cixi, was dead, and the powerful General Yuan Shikai had declared himself the new emperor. Forces throughout the country were battling over who would rule China's future. There was fighting around Tientsin and Peking, and, ever since the Boxer Uprising, the foreign-controlled enclaves had raised militias and were guarding their gates. Bandit gangs roamed the countryside. There was plague in Nanking. Thousands were homeless as a result of summer floods; farmlands were under water due to neglect of the dykes and riverbanks in the north. Starvation stalked the land. In essence, there was no central government and, always in the background, there was the threat of foreign intervention with the aim of further carving up Chinese territory. Even the British/American Compound and St. John's University in Shanghai were not immune to the violence and chaos.

On December 5th, 1915, Arch was coming out of the Sunday Vespers service when he heard the sound of heavy guns coming from the direction of the arsenal near the port. Arch climbed to the top floor of Yen Hall and could see flashes coming from ships in the harbor. He had been in China only a few months, but he knew what was happening. Shanghai was under attack.

St. John's University was located in the British/American settlement next to the French Compound. These Western concessions had been carved out of Chinese territory by various countries seeking access to China's rich resources, cheap labor, and trade. In fact, the West had been in the process of carving up China for more than half a century. Naturally these trading compounds, missionaries, and foreigners were hated by both the Manchu Qing dynasty and Chinese revolutionaries. Thus it was no accident that the resident westerners were hidden behind walls and guarded bridges.

Shortly after arriving in Shanghai, and in contrast to his idealistic Christian belief in love and justice, Arch Mitchell joined the well-armed Shanghai Volunteer Corps (the SVC of the journals). The Corps was a local militia composed of young teachers, missionaries, foreign businessmen, and Chinese Boy Scouts trained and led by British officers. Here was the raw face of imperialism, and it wasn't long before Private Mitchell had his first test under arms.

At 3:40 AM on December 5th, the principal of the school burst into Mitchell's room with the news that the SVC had been ordered to mobilize. Arch dressed and fetched his rifle and headed out to guard a bridge leading to the compound. He spent a cold night on duty, but the attack fell on the nearby French Compound and he did not see action.

As it turned out, the event was historically significant. The attack was led by none other than Chiang Kai-shek, who survived to later become the Generalissimo and leader of Nationalist China.

At twenty-four, Arch Mitchell was unaware of the broader historical importance of the critical events he was witnessing and in which he was a participant. But his journals graphically capture the events of vanishing old China. In addition to the five surviving journals, he left over nine hundred photo prints and lantern slides of those historic times.

From these fluent accounts and accompanying photos we get a firsthand look at the last days of China's ancient regime as it disappeared under the dust and dynamism of a modernizing world. The journals and photos describe and depict the thousands of grave mounds immediately outside Shanghai, ancient temples, Chinese farms, thousand-year-old bridges, beggars in the streets, pagodas, and canals crowded with junks, and, most graphically of all, the Chinese people themselves.

This was an intensely complex and chaotic period in Chinese history. The Boxer Uprising of 1899 to 1901 was not the only rebellion during this period but it is one of the best known in Western history because of its scale. Thirty-two-thousand Chinese Christians and 239 missionaries were murdered during the uprising and a long siege was laid on the Foreign Legations in Peking. This violence was followed by over a decade of local unrest, regional rebellions, threats of foreign intervention, and reparation payments. In particular, there were Republican efforts to radically challenge the Qing Dynasty, which was presided over by the conniving and evasive Dowager Empress, Cixi. Finally, in 1911, the two-hundred-year-old Manchu Qing Dynasty collapsed, ending 2,100 years of dynastic rule in China.

Change came when the powerful general Yuan Shikai, with his effective and well-armed northern army group (the Beiyang), joined forces with the southern Kuomintang under Sun Yat-sen. But any attempt to introduce democracy was shortlived. Sun was driven from power and Yuan continued his dictatorial rise. In 1915, in a foolish attempt to gain stability and prestige, he dissolved the Parliament and declared himself emperor, thereby provoking more conflicts.

After Yuan Shikai died in June 1916, China was thrown into a long period of political chaos and warlordism.

During this period, European business interests and Christian missionaries were exerting tremendous cultural and financial influence. They introduced modern Western ideas, which clashed with the traditional values of the former Manchu rulers. The conservative, land-rich gentry, who had sided with the Qing Dynasty, were in decline; powerful warlords amassed fortunes by squeezing their territories to support their local armies. Conflicts between provinces led to frequent uprisings, brush-fire wars, and suppression of the long-suffering population.

In 1916, during the reign of Yuan Shikai, Arch wrote a letter home to his sister Sue describing the conditions in which he lived. He wrote of the floods and famines, a nearby plague, local conflicts, armies on the move, rumors of foreign intervention and the fact that, in spite of it all, somehow "China functions...." The mail was delivered, the trains ran, the ancient canal systems carried on, and the rice crops were harvested just as they had been for the last forty centuries.

We can see in his journal and letters Arch's growing love for China and its tough, enduring people. Though he was an American who viewed the East through imperialistic spectacles, he nonetheless managed to record his experiences with sensitivity and objectivity. His spontaneous journals recount his travels and daily life in graceful, descriptive passages, some of which are reminiscent of Conrad and other contemporary voyagers. And although he occasionally gives free rein to his feelings, his aim is to distance himself from his personal struggles, and see, as he wrote, "things more from the outside."

His objective stance is maintained throughout, as he lucidly describes his numerous adventures, the places he visits, and the people he meets.

Even though he set out to write unbiased descriptions, there are examples of the imperialistic provincialism that characterized the period. When the text is clouded by prejudices, it must be remembered that Arch was still a young man, teaching English composition, literature, and banking to junior college-level Chinese students at a Christian missionary school. His own bias in favor of Christianity never quite slackened enough to admit the value of rival Buddhist traditions. Nevertheless, his curiosity led him to spend a great deal of time and effort visiting temples and holy sites, attending a local wedding, and visiting religious celebrations. The journals are enriched by his genuine appreciation of the colorful Buddhist culture and ultimately by his love for the Chinese people themselves.

In this edition of the journals, we have decided to leave in Arch's occasionally biased comments and use of now obsolete terms, such as "coolie", "tiffin", and "heathenish", rather than edit them out. This was, after all, 1915, over one hundred years ago, and an entirely different world. We decided to leave in the obsolete place names such as Peking and Canton and update them in a glossary. We also kept his capitalization, spelling and punctuation mostly intact.

Viewed from the perspective of our time, when China is once again moving through dramatic economic and political changes, and Shanghai is a buzzing high-rise metropolis, these journals offer a glimpse into the tremendous effort and struggles the Chinese people had to exert to win their future. Arch's descriptions of the vanishing face of old China during the turbulent period between the end of the Qing Dynasty and the foundation of the Republic are especially poignant, considering the violence to come from the Japanese attempt to conquer China in World War II, and the victories of the Communist Party and creation of the People's Republic of China in 1949.

One is reminded of Napoleon's admonition: "China is a sleeping

giant. Let her sleep, for when she wakes, she will move the world."
Arch Mitchell had no idea, of course, that he was recording the beginnings of that great awakening.

Hugh Powers Mitchell, Rochester, New York, 2017

The Journals of James Archibald Mitchell
China 1915 -1918

James A. Mitchell at The Great Wall with friends

J. A. Mitchell's chop

September 25, 1915,
An Incident at the Ferry, Shanghai

事変

Tonight we had the first real excitement since I arrived in China. I was reading *The Oxford Book of English Verse* and was just gathering my duds together preparatory to going over to Mann Hall to bed when we heard a strange noise. I remarked to my friend, Don, that there was another strange sound adding to the list the Chinese boys can make. But I had no sooner gotten the words out than the noise increased in intensity and we perceived that something unusual was happening. We rushed out on the back verandah and found students rushing from their rooms and everything in an uproar. I thought at first that one of the students was sick or had hurt himself but then noticed that the sounds came from the direction of the creek. There were loud, piercing shrieks and a jargon of baser voices in an uproar. My heart sank for I thought immediately that someone was drowning and the thought of that dirty water was enough to make one sick. I ran downstairs, found the gate to the playground locked and was obliged to climb over the high fence, and ran across the playground towards the sounds. But when I arrived at the ferry I soon saw no one was overboard — instead, there was a fight of some sort going on. Two boats were close together; men were pummeling on each other with poles and somewhere in the mass a woman was screaming. Evidently she was the point at issue and was getting the worst of it.

As I was debating to myself the best course to pursue (I was the only outsider to the quarrel as yet on the premises) another man arrived — one of the Chinese students — and ran out on the boat yelling to them in Chinese. I followed, and our arrival seemed to break up the party — at least they stopped fighting, although they continued to talk loudly and the woman continued to cry. (Up to this point I thought she was a child, but now I saw she was a woman.) About that time the crowd of students and faculty arrived in force and after much aimless talking and a good deal of loud Chinese and the necessary translation by one of the students, we found that a man (now in our custody) had been attempting to steal the wife of our ferryman. He had two others with him to help in the process and these three had been fighting with the ferryman, who was putting up a valiant fight in defense of his lawful property. The woman, half way between the boats, pulled now this way and now that and generally pummeled around, was yelling Billy Blue Murder for help. The poor thing was frightened to death and even after the fight was over she continued to weep in great sobs and was so excited she could not answer our questions. And no wonder — to be the center of a fight like that is not my idea of a good time!

The incident was closed by calling up the police and putting all three attackers under their custody. Three tall, black-bearded Sikhs came out to do the arresting. The coolies were very docile under these fierce looking officials and marched away quietly, tied queue to queue, and with the husband bringing up the rear to put in his accusation.

Ferry at Van-Waung-Doo

November 21, 1915
A Walk Along Soochow Creek
Toward Nanyang

野

A typical Autumn in China leaves nothing to be desired in the way of weather, and since this Autumn has been very chary in granting such days, when one does come it is a great incentive get out into the open fields. Such a day back in America would have smacked of football or of chestnutting, but in China meant the dry paths and a tingle to the blood and so two of us started out for a long walk through the crowded countryside.

Boats on Soochow Creek

Our initial route lay alongside one of China's great highways of commerce, a creek which connects two of her great cities and which for hundreds of years has been part of the great system of canals forming practically the only means of communication and transportation. Today, although the railroad has invaded the field, it has produced little or no effect upon this great commercial artery. Moreover, the perfection of steam and gas as a native power for vessels has changed but little the methods of transportation on the creek; the same methods of propulsion are used today as they have been for generations in the past. Great heavy junks with their great square sails, some of them reduced to rags, sail slowly along; small punts skim along sculled by one lone man; and between these two extremes are all sizes and descriptions of vessels, some sculled, some poled, some towed, but all of ancient pattern and construction.

When we left the well beaten tow path, which bordered this creek and struck off into the country, we did not, as one might suppose, leave behind all evidence of canals and water, instead, the tributaries of the creek seemed to follow us wherever we went and we were continually crossing and recrossing sluggish streams. Indeed, the whole countryside is an intricate design of land and streams and unless one stays on the beaten paths it is impossible to progress. "Cross-country" is out of the question. The paths themselves are scattered everywhere; they seem to lead to nowhere in particular and wind in and out in a most amazing manner. Nor are they "roads" in any sense of the term — simply paths through the country, beaten down into a semblance of hardness (in dry weather) by the feet of thousands and by the tracks of the wheelbarrows. Where they cross the many streams are little bridges made of long blocks of stone. Many of them are quite distinctive and they form the most picturesque part of the landscape.

Shanghai Country Scene: Stone Slab Bridge

4

As we walked briskly along these paths we had plenty of evidence (if we did not know it ourselves) that the day was a fine one. All the country people seemed to be outdoors, and when you speak thus of a countryside which is as thickly populated as any in the world, it means that you are continually in sight of someone. Many were enroute down our path. A bent old man would shuffle along, a young fellow on his way to the fields would stride by, another, loaded down by great buckets which swung from a pole over his shoulder, would chant in time with his footsteps as he swung along. Then too there were women and children in brightly colored clothes and caps who stared solemnly as we passed.

Presently there came a blind man walking rapidly and feeling his way with a long cane. We waited to watch him negotiate a turn in the path and were surprised at the ease with which he did it. Now came a man with two baskets swung over his shoulders; in one, a great bundle of rags and in the other, neatly balancing them, a sleeping baby. Behind him waddled the mother holding another child by the hand.

But these people were not the only evidence that the land was thickly populated, for throughout the whole countryside are the grave mounds and coffins and other evidences of the departed. Indeed, it is these mounds and coffins which one first notices about a Chinese landscape, and which create the main impression of the country. They are scattered everywhere and anywhere — literally this section of China is one great graveyard.

Grave Mounds in Shanghai Country

There are many forms of graves, perhaps the most common being a conical mound of earth about five feet high and the rarest a mere coffin laying exposed in the field. Some are vaults of brick with tiled roofs, others are coffins thatched with straw; many of the mounds contain six or a dozen bodies and are huge affairs, others contain children's bodies and are very small. The most elaborate grave mounds are surrounded by a moat and a hedge and have a grove of trees as an added luxury. Some even have a small temple nearby for the worship of the departed spirits, and we saw one which was fitted up nicely and was well kept; evidently the family used it as a sort of picnicking ground and Summer house.

Most of the graves were in a bad state of repair, nevertheless it was evident that they were highly respected.* Not one is encroached upon for crops and most of them have nearby a little pile of ashes where the spirits have been propitiated by the burning of paper money.

This same paper money was being made in great quantities in all the villages through which we passed, indeed it seemed to be the chief article of manufacture. It consists of cardboard, carefully covered with tinsel, so as to resemble coins or silver bullion.

I have said that the graves are scattered through the countryside, perhaps I should have said that around and among the graves are scattered the fields. There are no fences in China, a man owns and cultivates a tiny plot of ground and he knows every inch of it. The size of these plots would make an American farmer smile. It would take a great many of them to make him think it worth the plowing. Yet the Chinese prosper on such tiny holdings. They manage this by intense cultivation and by practicing the strictest economy. We saw the farmers pulling up the dried cotton stalks to use as fuel, but even before they were dried out, bean stalks were taking their place. That same piece of land would yield many crops during the year.

The one useful purpose of the grave mounds is to furnish grass. We saw many goats feeding on them and a few ungainly water buffalo. These massive brutes are used for plowing, and for their milk. It is said that they do not like foreigners and often chase them – they have some objection to our smell it is believed! But we passed quite close to a number of them and they did not bother us.

* see End Notes

The only animals which objected to our presence were the dogs, who are also said to object to Western smell. They heralded our entrance at every hamlet, but on sight of our walking sticks beat a hasty retreat and even became silent. So necessary is a cane for this purpose when walking in the China countryside that canes have come to be called in Chinese a "hit-dog-stick."

The little villages and the groups of country houses were interesting places. Chinese houses are entirely open in front and so you get a full view of all that is going on. As we passed through we were greeted with stares by the men and women and by joyful cries by the children. They would all come running and invariably the cry was for money; some said "doong-ba, doong ba" (coppers,) others were more ambitious and cried out "yang-dien" (dollar); and one bunch even knew the English word and said "da-la." They think all foreigners are rich. Some few children were in school and as we passed. We could hear them chanting their lessons, each one at the top of his voice and each saying a different thing.

Eventually we were clear of the groups of houses and the little groves of bamboo which are grown at the end of each house, and once more were in the open country — the country of winding paths, of little creeks, stone bridges and graves. But it is all very flat and deceptive and of a sudden a foreign house popped before our eyes, we stepped on to a macadamized road and a motorcar honked by! We were back again in "civilization."

Boats, Bridges, and Canals

Shanghai Harbor

Soochow Creek

Two Junks

Soochow Creek

Canal Boat Children

Water Gate in City Wall

Bridge over Wusih Canal

Typical Stone Bridge near Shanghai

Canal Scene

Saturday, December 4, 1915
The Paper Hunt
(see End Notes)

狩猎

We had made up a riding party of five or six for this afternoon but at the last minute and for various reasons all backed out except Miss Jo Graves and myself. So we resolved to go at any rate.

About 2:30 the "mofoo" or guide, came with ponies and we started. This was my first time on a horse since I went down into the Grand Canyon (and that "horse" had been a mule!) so it seemed very strange at first. In addition, the horses used are mere ponies from Manchuria and my particular one showed his disposition by nipping at me when I rubbed his nozzle and playfully kicking when I started to get on.

The gate of these beasts was an uncomfortable trot, and having never learned to post properly I was very awkward. But at a faster pace, my pony had a most delightful and easy canter. So I tried to make him canter all the time, much to his disgust.

Our mofoo suggested that we ride over in the country towards the south, as a paper hunt was scheduled for that afternoon. We gladly did so, and were surprised to find a constantly increasing stream of automobiles, carriages, and horseback riders. Evidently the hunt was to be quite an affair. And so it proved to be.

There must have been at least thirty to forty riders ready for the start and, save for the fact that the dogs were lacking, the scene resembled the start of a huge fox hunt. There were all sorts and descriptions of costumes, a few red coats and jockey's hats lending a touch of color and atmosphere, and the horses varied from tall splendid looking fellows, to hardy little ponies such as we were riding.

At a given word these horsemen were off with a rush, following a trail of paper which led across the open fields, across ditches, around and among grave mounds and off into the flat cultivated land. We had stationed ourselves along with other spectators at the first ditch, to see if perchance, as our mofoo expressed it, "Two or three pieces might take fall." There were a number of horsemen looking on, a greater number of Shanghai's English 400 on foot, and an even greater crowd of Chinese, who stood on the grave mounds of their ancestors and gazed with great amazement and interest at the strange doings of the foreigners. No accidents happened at the first ditch, so the crowd dispersed and made posthaste for the finish of the race a mile or so down the road. There was a great crush of automobiles and horsemen on the road but all finally arrived safely and took up their position to see the end.

The Paper Hunt

The trail of paper here led between four red flags and just before these flags was a wide ditch with perpendicular sides which all the riders would have to jump. We waited some time, and finally the cry arose "Here they come." And here they did come, strung out in a great line with groups of two or three together, and winding in and out among the mounds with great speed as they urged their horses for the finish. A man on a white pony and dressed picturesquely in one of the red coats led the field and he leaped the ditch successfully and finished first amidst the cheers of the many spectators.

Then they continued to pour in, leaping the gap as they came — it was a magnificent sight. Only one horse balked and one horse came in riderless — so there were no real accidents.

We rode home at a good clip, for the ponies were excited at all the racing and noise and wanted to race everyone we passed, as well as each other. It was a splendid afternoon and I can pronounce my first ride in China an unqualified success.

Sunday, December 5, 1915
Trouble in Shanghai
(see End Notes)

G reat excitement tonight!
About seven, as we were coming out of church, the sound of heavy guns could be heard from the direction of the arsenal. From the top of Yen Hall the flashes could also be seen, which verified the fact that the firing was in fact the sound of guns. But no one thought much of it, merely wondered why they should be firing.

After dinner about eight, I was about to go to the library, when Dr. Lincoln's fraulein appeared at the door with white, frightened face and rapped sharply. We opened the door and she poured forth a torrent of broken English about telephones, Norton, the Volunteer Corps*, and the like. Immediately we connected it with the gun fire and thought the Corps had been called out and it turned out there was trouble in the native city, refugees were arriving in the Settlement, the Corps had been ordered to "stand by," and Norton was to get his troupe of Boy Scouts ready for carrying messages on their bicycles. I gave orders to Chung Loh, and proceeded to get into my SVC uniform.

Then the real excitement began; the boys were aroused and the foreigners also alarmed and were trying to find out some definite news by phoning. But no one could find anything out, the police did not answer, and our squad leader had had no orders to mobilize.

Finally, a message came to Headquarters informing us of trouble in the native city with orders to the SVC to stand by and be ready to be called. Mr. Ely came back from a flying trip to town in his car and reported but little excitement, a crowd at the entrance to the native city, policemen with bayonets holding them at bay, vague rumors of an attack on the arsenal, but no real evidence of an uprising.

So the excitement gradually subsided and we had to wait until to-

* see End Notes for more about the Shanghai Voluteer Corps (SVC)

morrow to find out what it was all about. I have an idea it will prove to be nothing but riots on the part of hungry rickshaw coolies, for they have been on a strike for the last few days and there have been many arrests and some trouble. But everywhere there is talk of the Monarchy Movement. The paper today reported a rumor that Yuan Shi-kai was to be crowned at New Year time and some think that may have started the trouble. At any rate we can only await developments, so I shall now doff my uniform and to bed.

Wednesday, December 8, 1915

The excitement of Sunday evening did not end so tamely as did my account. During the night (Sunday) we heard further firing of heavy guns. It turned out there had been a small rebellion. About six-thirty a number of men came down the river in a launch and ran alongside the Chinese cruiser *Chao Ho*. They jumped aboard with drawn pistols and ordered the crew to surrender. The crew had already been notified of the coming trouble and joined the rebels with alacrity. The few officers on board (most of them were away at a dinner) were taken prisoner. Then the rebels signaled the other cruiser to join her in an assault on the arsenal. On her refusal, the rebels started to bombard the cruiser. That was the firing we heard.

I had some errands to do in town so I went in that afternoon hoping to see some excitement and get further news. Everything was quiet and business was going on as usual. The newspapers reported that during the night the captured cruiser had been bombarded by the arsenal and the rebels had evacuated and many had been captured. Furthermore, the paper reported that the government troops had the situation in hand and everything was quiet.

All this was based upon a statement by the Chinese Commander, however, so was not thoroughly believed. During the firing the night before, a number of houses in the Settlement had been struck, but fortunately the shells were not explosive ones and hence had done little harm. Eleven shells in all fell in the Settlement.

On Monday night as I went to bed, I heard further firing, more indeed that on the previous night, and my last thought on going to sleep was that we had not seen the last of this trouble as yet. I was right.

About 3:40 A.M. Dr. Lincoln burst into my room with the news that the SVC had been ordered to mobilize and I was to report at once. It is not a very pleasant thing to be called up in the coldest part of the night and the fact that you may have to fight in an hour or so does not add to the fun. I got into my uniform and fighting equipment. Soon Norton came over and we started off. Just outside the gate there is a bicycle shop, so we hammered on the door, made the poor Chinaman get out of bed and lend us wheels. He demurred at first, saying the owner was out of town, but on sight of our uniforms he moved a little quicker and even went so far as to file the off chain that locked the wheels in the shop. We started in town, passing a few early birds on their way to work, some of the night rickshaw coolies and a few Sikh police.

JAM on Requisitioned Bicycle

As we approached the city proper we passed a file of British SVC and from then on were constantly meeting pickets. The military was out in force.

We reported at the Victoria Fire Station and were given ammunition and appointed to a squad. My group soon marched off for duty and I found myself guarding the Szechuan bridge over Soochow Creek. It was easy work, for traffic was very light and in spite of the time of year and the hour, 5 AM, it was not very cold. We have had a warm spell for a week — beautiful Autumn weather.

My guard time was short and on being relieved I went with the rest of the squad to a cork factory nearby to rest. There was a squad of the Italian Company there also and we had some talk about the trouble. Rumor held that there was an attempt to blow up the French Police Station with bombs and that there had been considerable fighting.

About six our squad was relieved and daybreak found us eating bread and jam and drinking coffee at the Fire Station. About seven, orders came from headquarters to demobilize and so we were dismissed, with orders to stand by and be ready to be called at any time. Norton and I wheeled back to college, and arrived in time for breakfast.

Afterward I had a shave and bath and attended my regular classes all day, a play rehearsal in the afternoon, and worked on the next day's classes until dinner.

The next day's paper reported that the trouble was a land attack on the arsenal and on several police stations. The rebels were driven back toward the Settlement, and on approaching the line they had encountered the French police. There was considerable firing and the rebels scattered, entered the Settlement, and began a street warfare and firing from houses. So the SVC was ordered out and it was only after much trouble that the rebels were ejected from the Settlement. About a dozen men were killed in all.

The whole revolt seemed to be backed by considerable money and caused by dissatisfaction with the way the Monarchy Movement is progressing. There is danger that it may assume greater proportions, though so far no trouble has been reported in the interior. The real fear is that the disturbance be taken by Japan as an excuse for intervention.

February 12, 1916
Hong Kong to Canton

香港

The South China Sea did not live up to its reputation and we had a very quiet trip across to Hong Kong, sighting land early the second morning. The weather had changed and instead of the mid-Summer of Manila*, it was very chilly and damp. The disagreeableness was further added to by the slowness of the British officials, for although we were outside the harbor entrance by eight o'clock, it was long after tiffin before they had finished their examination of the ship and passengers and would allow us to land. My friend Frank Samuel met us on the tender and we put ourselves under his guidance while tending to baggage, engaging passage to Canton, and getting permits to leave the city and so forth.

Hong Kong

* Arch visited Manila for four days before proceeding to Hong Kong.

20

Hong Kong is a very distinctive and beautiful city. The harbor itself is one of the most wonderful I have seen, being completely landlocked and surrounded by high hills and mountains. We did not see it under the most advantageous conditions, but even at that, it was magnificent. The entrance seemed to be well guarded, forts and guns could be seen and the hillsides were honeycombed with passages. And moreover, as this was war time, the whole outer harbor was spotted with mines, which could be located by the flags above them. The city of Victoria, which most people confuse as Hong Kong proper, is located chiefly along the water's edge at the foot of a great mountain. But the houses are not confined to the harbor, for they straggle up over the whole mountain called "the Peak" and in hot weather it forms the Mecca for all the inhabitants. It is this remarkable location on a mountainside which gives the city its beauty. Even within the city itself, however, it's remarkably beautiful for the East. The buildings are tall, all with verandas and have arches on every floor; there are flowers in profusion and the streets are wide and clean. Many of the streets are so steep that they are in steps and the only traffic is on foot and in sedan chairs. Walking these streets is like climbing stairs.

Hong Kong, being a British colony, is typically British in every way and so we found the stores, the people and the general atmosphere but little different from Shanghai. The fact that it is now a belligerent in both Europe and also the Irish uprising was evident. We saw soldiers galore, had to use our passports to get in and to get a special pass to go to Canton.

Samuel, two others, and myself took the night steamer for Canton that same day.

February 14, 1916

I write on a river steamer enroute to Canton. It is a Chinese steamer, new, fast and remarkably clean, and in many ways is a most interesting boat. *Tai Lee* is the name and she makes the trip down the Pearl River twice each day, a deed only possible because of her speed. Furthermore, she is the cheapest one of the river boats, the cabin down being only $3.00 Canton silver, and they gave us an excellent dinner tonight for $1.25. But the most interesting part of the boat are the officers. They are all foreigners, chiefly British from their talk and to me a most unusual set of men. There seems to be much more to them than to ordinary officers on a steamer and certainly they far exceed what you would expect on a Chinese river steamer. One of them told me fascinating tales of Chinese pirates, of executions, of their cruelty, and chatted as familiarly of the Amazon and of Alaska as of the Pearl River.

Another officer next to me at the table talked of political conditions in China and the next minute switched to Dickens, then back to American politics. But enough of this boat. I have been living through five far more interesting days than this boat could possibly give, for I have just been in that quaint, ancient city of Canton.

Canton Christian College

During my stay in Canton I was visiting Frank Samuel, a fellow from Kansas whom I met on the *Nippon Maru* and who has been teaching at Canton Christian College for three and a half years.

The college was in session during only two days of my stay but I had plenty of opportunity to see the buildings themselves. They impress me as particularly well-built and well-adapted to the needs of an institution of the kind. The grounds, however, are in a very bad state and there is no shade. While I was there it was cool. In fact, Samuel and

22

others who have been in this hot climate for years and whose blood is therefore thin, insisted it was very cold, but in Summer it must be unbearably hot.

The faculty seems to be very good and the whole compound a most companionable bunch, though of course not of the elite in a social way. They were very kind to me and we were out for nearly every meal except breakfast during the five or six days I was there. Indeed one day we got up before sunrise, rode some miles across the island forded the river in a Chinese "slipper boat" and had breakfast with some friends of Samuel's, the Pagets of Harrisburg.

The college is located on a hill on an island south of the city and is about the highest spot in the city, being the only place above high water in the recent flood. The island itself is about eleven miles long and four wide and is a most interesting place. We rode over much of it on the tiny ponies they use and saw something of the village and country life of south China. It is quite different from that around Shanghai. The graves are in the shape of very small mounds and have stones to mark them or else they are great "horseshoe" ones of granite and cement. They are even thicker than those around St. John's for this island being high is a favorite burying place of the Chinese. The college itself was built on what used to be a graveyard. The fields are not so tiny as ours and they seem to be even better cultivated. However, there is much more waste land in the form of bamboo groves and ponds or what used to be ponds and this, combined with the hills, tends to make the country much prettier than ours. The villages are of stone and have granite paved streets. Many have fine temples and other interesting features. The people impress me as more intelligent and less miserable than those in the north. Even the dogs reflect this greater prosperity. They are "chows," very good looking and since they range freely over the countryside they remind me of wolves. The children are a happy lot, not as dirty as our poor kids and less inclined also to beg for money.

The most striking thing on the island is a huge eleven story pagoda, which towers over the whole country side and which is so ancient that it is crumbling away. The earth thus produced from the mud bricks is growing trees from the seeds dropped by birds!

Canton Pagoda

Every day there I have spent time visiting Canton, riding horseback in the country, rowing on the river. I found it all so fascinating; from the morning when we rolled out of our bunks on the river steamer and took the launch down the river to the college, to this afternoon, when, just before sailing, we saw a squad of soldiers march by leading a file of pirates to be shot at the North Gate.

Taking Pirates to be Shot

One hears so often of the dirt and smells of Canton, and of the misery of the boat life, and the narrowness and filthiness of the streets, that that is the main thing for which you look on first seeing the city. Strangely enough my impressions were just the opposite. When we first landed I looked hard for wretched conditions in the boats on the river and I could not see any. Then when we first went into the city itself I expected to find the most horrible filth and unbearable smells. It was still comparatively clean, and so it proved throughout. Canton is dirty, and the streets do smell, and are narrow, but I suppose that I have become so accustomed to all of that, that it is almost second nature to me. And in any case, Canton cannot hold a candle to Nanking as to filth and I am sure that even our little village of Zou Ka Doo can surpass it as to smells.

Canton River Boats

The boats of Canton are perhaps its most distinctive feature and the thing that everyone remembers and speaks of when mentioning Canton. The boats line both sides of the river for a great distance and are packed side-by-side a dozen or more thick. There are many varieties too, from the gaily colored huge "passage boats" to the small

25

sampans which form the greater percent. As I have said I was struck by the cleanliness of these boats and of the boat people. We crossed in them a number of times and found the boats themselves washed spotless and the men and women who rowed them comparatively clean and certainly happy and seemingly well fed. They have none of the wretchedness of apparel and of face which marks our Soochow Creek boat people in Shanghai. Moreover, at flood time (and incidentally they are still talking of the recent flood in Canton) they are certainly the safest in all the city and reap great harvests from transporting their less fortunate land-bound neighbors.

The streets of Canton are also notable for the heights of the buildings that line them and for the pavements. They are more like canyons than streets and this simile is well borne out in that they are paved with granite blocks, worn smooth and slippery by the bare feet of millions of pedestrians over the centuries. Naturally, the narrow thoroughfares are full to the brim with traffic, though all of it must is on foot. There are carriers with their bamboo poles laden down with strange burdens, and there are numerous sedan chairs borne on the shoulders of coolies who call out with their strange shouts of warnings and add to the jargon of other street sounds. Occasionally, too there are ponies, but rickshaws or other vehicles are not possible on the narrow streets.

One smell in Canton which predominates is that of incense. Before each shop is a little vault of brick in which sticks of junk are always burning, lending a fragrance to the street that is not unpleasant and helps kill some of the worse odors. The smell reminds me more of the China I had imagined than anything I have yet seen or smelt.

The stores themselves are very well kept and seem well stocked. The various goods are sold according to kind in certain sections, that is to say certain streets are devoted to shops of a certain goods and to those goods only. For example, there is a shoe street, an ivory street, a blackwood street, a junk street etc. I was delighted with these shops, for I have never before seen such beautiful Chinese goods. We spent a great deal of time shopping and I fear too much money. In our various trips to the different streets and shops I picked up a number of curios and still more presents for next Christmas, including some beautiful linen and silk embroidery, carved ivory, a blackwood bench, and an opium pipe. Samuel also gave me an old idol he had obtained from some Yomen at the time of the Second Revolution and which had originally been in one of the temples in Canton.

We saw a number of temples in our sightseeing. Among them was that of the 500 Genji. It is notable for its size. You come upon it in the midst of the closely packed city and it is seemingly but a small affair tucked away in a corner, but when once within its gate the courtyards and passages seem endless. There are at least 500 idols and among them is a statue of Marco Polo! Another temple was that of the five Genji that has a huge bell out of which the French chipped a piece when they held the city.

There is a beautiful view of the city from the tower of this temple too, but on the day we were there, it was murky. Still another sightseeing spectacle is that of the ancient water clock which has marked time by dripping water for centuries. Of more human interest than the clock were the miserable beggars who droned for alms beneath the gateway in which the clock is located.

But the greatest temple of all is that of the family. It has been but recently erected, was forty years in building and is remarkable for its carvings. Never have I seen such magnificent or painstaking work and our fellow travelers, Mr. and Mrs. Ely, who have accompanied us in most of our sightseeing and have been all over the world, said the same thing about it.

"Shameen," the Foerign Concession

A description of Canton and my visit there is not complete without a mention of Shameen and of the Canton Christian College. Shameen is the foreign settlement of Canton. It is situated on an island in the river and has some very beautiful residences, wide streets, great banyan trees and many other European features which stand in vivid contrast to the native city. Its most unusual feature to me was the fact that the wide, tree lined streets were not used as streets at all, for there is no traffic and no use for traffic. Grass grows in nearly all the thoroughfares. Indeed, in all Canton there is no traffic in our sense of the word; there are two carriages on the Bund and two automobiles, which the authorities will not allow to run.

Tiffin in a Cantonese Restuarant

My most enjoyable experience in Canton was tiffin at a Chinese restaurant. I never have eaten such delicious food, and the restaurant itself was a most interesting place. The entrance was unimposing, but the higher we went in the building the better it was fitted up, for with the Chinese, the finest food is obtained on the highest floor. My first course was sharks' fin soup and though I tackled it with some trepidation I was soon smacking my lips and wishing there was more. It is a most delicious dish and unlike anything I have eaten before. Then came what we called "chicken mien," a hot indescribable mass of meat, flat macaroni, and other things I could not name. It was excellent but very hard to eat, especially since I am not yet accustomed to chopsticks. The final dish and by far the best was roast duck. The taste of that well-turned thin crackling lingers with me yet. The duck was roasted whole and then cut into very thin slivers which almost melted in your mouth. Later the rest of the bird including even the bill was brought in just to show us that we had a whole duck! There were various strange accessories to the tiffin, including watermelon seeds, tea, hot water, various sauces, betel gum to clean our teeth, and at the very end, basins full of hot scented water and a towel with which we were to remove the debris from our faces.

I am delighted with south China and Canton and leave it with regret. I fancy it must bear something of the relation to Shanghai and Peking that our beloved Southland does to New England.

Views of Canton

Canton Village Street

Beggar on City Street

Horseshoe Grave

Opium Bench

Loading Boats, Canton Harbor

The Bund

April 11, 1916
Scout trip to Kunshau
(see End Notes)

童子軍

most interesting weekend: Three of us foreigners, Norton, Don Roberts, and myself, and about fourteen students, all "Boy Scouts," had a two-day camping trip.

We left by the afternoon train on Saturday after a great deal of excitement getting prepared and after tiffin. Travelling on a Chinese train is in itself an experience and especially so when you are travelling Third Class, as we did. The seats run lengthwise and there are four rows of them: four rows of smelly, tightly packed, ever talking and ever eating Chinese humanity.

Outside it was a beautiful Spring day, and as we rolled through the flat country with its small green fields, its creeks and ponds, and its multitudes of grave mounds, it had a beauty I had never appreciated before. What made it particularly so was the yellow rape which was overgrowing the whole countryside and the long cotton streamers with which nearly all the graves were adorned. It looked as though this was a season of rejoicing.

We reached Kunshau, our destination, in good time (about one hour from Shanghai) and disembarked with our nineteen bundles and bags. Coolies were summoned, and after much arguing and shouting and gesticulating, they loaded themselves and were off down a long stretch of brick highway to the city.

Norton, one of the Assistant Scoutmasters (a Chinese man) and myself separated from the bunch and went in search of the chief official of the city for permission to camp. We first went to the home of a catechist of our church to get his assistance in interpreting, as well as the advantage of his prestige. He was not at home but a great crowd of his children and grandchildren were there, and we were received with great curiosity. His wife (at least I suppose she was his wife) and daughter-in-law received us courteously, asked us to sit and wait while they sent a child for the catechist, and offered us tea. So we sat in the little house opening on the courtyard and waited. Eventually the old gentleman came and after explanations, we left the house (where by this time the daughter had become so accustomed to us that she even fed the baby in our presence!) and under his guidance went to the governor's yomen. We had letters to the official from Dr. Pott and armed with these we sailed past the soldiers at the outer gate, the soldiers at the inner gate, presented them to a servant and waited. Presently along came some official whom I took to be the governor. There was much bowing and scraping and much talking in the strange local dialect, and everything seemed to be fixed up all right. This official, it seems, was the chief of police, for the governor had no intention of leaving his evening meal to bother with us, but the chief gave us permission to camp and even insisted upon sending two soldier-police to protect us. He further invited us to sit in the yomen* (a most polite invitation) but as our business was ended we declined with thanks and were off for the prospective camp.

Coolie with Camping Gear in Kunshau

* see Glossary. In this case, Arch is probably referring to the yomen's "office."

Kunshau gets its name from the fact that very near it, and indeed included in its ancient city walls, is a high rocky hill. This hill is of most peculiar geologic formation, rising as it does precipitately out of a great flat country and being the only elevation for scores of miles around. It was on this hill that our camp was located, and by the time we had passed through the narrow city streets and climbed the steep path, we found that the tents had already been pitched. By this time, it was dusk and it gave one a most peculiar sensation to stand on this high eminence and look on three sides into the dark, where you felt rather than saw the great lowland country stretching out.

After many delays we got supper cooked and were so hungry that we did not at all object to the dirt that was cooked with it. In the meantime, two soldiers had come trailing up the hill lighting their way with a great paper lantern, and had taken up a position nearby as our protectors. They were good-natured fellows dressed in a neat blue uniform and seemed much amused at our camp. Presently too, came another lantern, and a Buddhist priest in the robes of his office and with a most vile garlic breath, emerged from the dark. He was the guardian of a small temple we had passed on our way up and turned out to be a most congenial old fellow and very helpful to us. From his place we obtained water, he treated us to tea, and on the next day we even cooked our rice on his stove, indeed I hardly think we could have gotten along without his assistance.

As we ate our supper we had another set of visitors, some northern soldiers who were quartered in the city below. They wore light yellow uniforms and they too were very good-natured fellows. Soon after supper as we played games around our campfire, more soldiers came. They brought a letter from their Captain telling us not to blow our bugle, as we had disturbed them and indeed frightened them. These are troublous times and the northern soldiers were in fact quartered in hostile territory, so naturally they are nervous.

We slept, or tried to sleep, that night stretched crosswise in the tents, nine to each tent, but I was none too sorry when morning came. But I was sorry when rain came with the morning. It was a light showery rain at first and between showers we cooked breakfast, did our camp duties, visited the Buddhist temple, had morning service and Bible study, took pictures and played Boy Scout games.

The scene from the hill in the daytime was magnificent. On all sides stretched the great lowland country of the Yangtze valley. It lay in rectangular patches of various colors, some green, some yellow, some brown, divided in parts by ponds and canals, and scattered with many little thatched villages. At the foot of our hill and winding about it was a fairly large creek, bounded on the nearside by a crumbling old wall. On one side lay the city of Kunshau with its white walls and dark tile roofs.

The extreme top of the hill was crested by an old crumbling pagoda rising from the midst of a well-kept and most interesting temple. This latter was well filled with idols of all descriptions and tended by a number of priests. Half way down the hill was another smaller, white temple — and here our old monk held sway. The hill was further notable for a number of caves and deep holes in the rocks, one cave in particular being very large and used to contain a number of idols which are now headless and hence (I presume) useless.

Visitors to the Camp outside Kunshau

Before dinner time we became the center of a large and admiring group of natives of the city. They stood around our tents to the number of about 150, with their eyes wide and their mouths busy making remarks upon our strange appearance and ways. Old men and working men, young women, boys and girls, even dowagers in their rich sedan

36

chairs flocked up the hill to see the circus. If ever I am free of the staring, curious glances of crowds of local people, I shall never more myself stare at uncouth mortals. When I leave China I shall be a fit subject for a sideshow, and will no doubt feel disappointed and uneasy when I attract no attention in America!

However, a little after dinner the rain began to fall in earnest and the crowd soon scattered. But it continued to rain, and so we were obliged to strike our tents, pack our duds and walk the three miles to the station in the midst of the worst of it. We were all soaked, dead tired, and hungry when we reached St. John's, but nevertheless the trip was pronounced a decided success.

Boy Scouts at the Pagoda

May 6, 1916
Soochow

苏州

Today I added another Chinese city to the list of those I have seen — Soochow.

In many ways it is a typical Chinese city and has all those characteristics for which they are notable — the same narrow, filthy streets, the same noisy, dirty crowds, the same open shops, the same goods, and strange looking foodstuffs for sale, the same flea bitten dogs, the same gaily clad, dirty children, and in fact the same odors, sights and sounds as are common in this strange old country. But Soochow is distinctive because of its water. Interspersed among its narrow, twisting streets and scattered over the whole city are canals — some wide, some very narrow, all dirty and all laden with craft. These canals are crossed by stone bridges which rise in the form of high arches and convert the streets into veritable hunchbacks. Because of these obstructions, travel in the crowded streets becomes even more of a dilemma than is the case in other Chinese cities. The problem is solved by the use of sedan chairs (which can go most anywhere) and by donkeys. I have used a good many conveyances in my life and some of them have been most pleasing ones, but for real excitement and pleasure and sport I have yet to find the equal of a donkey ride through Soochow streets. The little beasts have on their back a huge apparatus resembling a mattress and on this you enthrone yourself, put your feet in two very short stirrups which double you up until you feel like Ichabod Crane, and grasp in your hand a dirty cloth rope which represents the reins. Behind you stands the owner of the beast, an ill-kempt coolie as odd-looking as his animal and in his hand is a whip. With a crack of this latter and a volley of yells, calls, hoots and imprecations from his well-developed lungs you are off. If you happen to be in a cavalcade (as we were) there will be donkeys in front and behind you, and alongside each beast will be his shouting, swearing master.

There is no chance for the cavalcade to slow down with these voices and whips to goad them into action, and personally I do not believe they would at any rate. Through the narrow crowded streets we were jostled, bounced, and slid with amazing speed: now we scraped against a post or around a corner, now we ran through a street restaurant, now we pushed a woman and child against a wall, now we careened from side to side and bumped children, and old men, dogs, and sedan chairs. And through all this confusion as we ploughed through, like a ship through a troubled sea, arose the strident yells of our coolies, the cracks of their whips, and the jangle of the bells with which each donkey was liberally supplied.

Bridge Near Soochow Hills

June, 1916
A Night at the Theater, Shanghai

戏剧

S ome time ago a number of us went to a Chinese theatre. Not the old style theatre that you read about in books, for they have practically disappeared in modern Shanghai, but a purely Chinese theatre which presented the weirdest adaptation of Old China to Western methods and manners. The whole thing, the building, the play, and acting was an attempt to copy the West; but as is usual when any attempt is made to copy manners and customs of another culture, the imitation presented only the most artificial side and was consequently so crude and at the same time ostentatious, as to be almost repellent to our Western eyes.

The things that saved it from this and gave it instead a most humorous side, were the Chinese customs and stage methods which still prevailed in the midst of the Western imitations. The theatre itself was an illustration of all this, for in an effort to outdo the West, the builder made the stage tremendous — next to the Hippodrome I believe it is larger than any in New York. The theatre itself is wider than it is long, but except for two tiny but very gaudy boxes, the stage is almost as wide as the theatre. Moreover, it has an apron that extends far into the audience, footlights and head lights that are marvels, a curtain which as an advertising medium would make Polis' pale in comparison, and a stock of scenery which would do justice to the finest theatre at home. We were fortunate in knowing the manager, and he showed us all the internal workings of the vast plant, enlarging all the while upon the number of men employees, the splendid equipment he had, and the spectacular effects he could — and did — produce.

The body of the theatre catered more to Chinese tastes, for in front of each line of seats was a narrow tiled table on which were set tea and eatables: watermelon seeds, sugar cane, water chestnuts and bananas. During the performance the lights did not go out in the body of the theatre, nor did the audience stop eating and chatting. It was very much like our cabaret shows. A further concession to Chinese tastes was the movie. The musicians — I hesitate to use that word — were seated on the stage itself on a sort of side apron, and between scenes they emitted that deafening clamor of gongs and drums and cymbals which the Chinese so love.

But the play itself was the richest of all. It was a detective story of the most hair-raising type, abounding in murders, villains, accomplices, stealth, masks, marques and policemen. It seems that every other character was a detective, even the murderer and his helpers, were detectives. So it was a battle of wits between detectives, a situation giving full rein to the author's ingenuity. And I suppose that every Chinese in the audience thought he was seeing a typical Western play!

There is no doubt but that the Chinese are born actors. The way they entered into the spirit of that play was inspiring. Moreover, there were some little touches which seemed to indicate that they were capable of a much finer kind of acting. To a certain extent they burlesqued this play — at least they made us all laugh when we should have shed tears. But of course they did not do it because they thought the play absurd. They did it simply "to get a laugh." And the costumes! the attempted Western manners, and the properties! I believe that whenever one character met another, even if they had separated but five minutes before, there was a solemn handshake. I wonder if we do use that manner of salutation as often and as absurdly as their observations would seem to indicate? The love glances too were rich, and perhaps best of all was a ball-room scene with which the play opened — a thing difficult enough for us Westerners to stage correctly.

Men played the women's parts and played them even more absurdly than do our college men, for they used the high falsetto which they are accustomed to use in Chinese plays. Moreover, they were overdressed and had squeezed themselves into such strange shapes, and the paint was on so thickly, that they resembled the worst type of wax manikins that you see in clothing store windows. Much of the action of the piece was conducted in accordance with Chinese stage etiquette. For instance, in a dialogue of any sort, both participants talked to the audience and not to each other. And if there was a soliloquy, the actor made no pretence but simply come down to the footlights and confidentially told the audience all about it. Much of the plot was entirely dependent upon information received in this way. There was no time wasted in the change of scenes. Two of the characters engaged in conversation at the time the scene was supposed to end, simply stepped forward to the front of the stage, the vivid advertising curtains were drawn behind them, and they continued with their conversations. On such occasions a coolie acting as property man always dragged a small table and two chairs to the center of the stage to give an atmosphere of reality to the scene. Then this coolie would stay there in view of the audience until it was time for the curtains to part and the table to be removed. I think we must have had a dozen changes of scene in the play, and each set seemed to surpass the other in magnificence. It was on this part that the management particularly prided itself. The last scene of all was a fitting climax to all their attempts and to the play itself. It represented a mountain glen at nightfall, with a great cliff in the near background, a winding path to its top, and at its foot a great pool, nay, two pools of real water. And from this cliff our detective hero was thrown bound and gagged into the lake below. But like all real heroes he burst his bonds and swam to safety, to wit: one set of painted rocks.

By this time, it was 12:30 A.M., so we all went home.

The next week they advertised an even more magnificent spectacle — a train was to be blown up on a great railroad bridge!

October 9, 1916
Chinese Wedding, Shanghai

结婚

I was most fortunate today in having an opportunity to attend an old fashioned Chinese wedding. Not that such weddings are rare now in China, but we who are thrown with the modern, educated Chinese are not often in a position to witness them. The one today was semi old-fashioned because the parents of the groom (Yuen Kung-tsao) live far in the interior, in Szechuan, are rather conservative, and particularly requested their son to have an old-style wedding. So in spite of the fact that the bride-to-be is a Christian, the ceremony was most heathenish indeed.

We arrived early at the typical Chinese city house with its noisy and smelly surroundings, and were shown through a lower room decorated in red and gold, up a narrow steep stairway to the apartments of the young couple-to-be. There seemed to be no other guests on hand, but there were plenty of round-eyed children and staring Chinese women. The rooms upstairs were lavishly decorated with all sorts of red and gaily-colored streamers, rosettes, and ribbons. On small tables were set bowls of fruits and candy, silver dishes, spoons and chopsticks, and various other ornaments, all securely tied to the furniture with red string. (It is a rule at a Chinese wedding that you may run away with anything you find lying loose!) At one end of the gaily decorated main room was a pile of beautifully embroidered quilts and pillows, scattered about it were various articles of furniture all securely sealed with red papers bearing the bride's name (in this case, Wong), and at the other end, forming the chief article and center of attraction, was the great bridal-bed. It was in reality only a very nice large foreign brass bed, but you could not see the foreign brass for the hangings and decorations. Over the whole was a panoply of silk partly consisting of beautiful embroidery, and further adorning it were various strange figures of silk, tinsel, silver and streamers. Each had its significance but we made no attempt to learn what they all meant, though I did catch that the greatest and central one was a figure bringing the good fortune of many children.

We sat around in this gay bridal chamber for about an hour waiting for the bride to come. In the meantime, we were entertained by tea, cakes, and candy, and by the bridegroom himself, who appeared in foreign afternoon dress and was attended by three young gentlemen likewise attired (most inappropriately, I thought). Finally, the outland-ish noise of a Chinese band was heard and we all adjourned to receive the bride. She came in a sedan chair gay with the bridal red, and at-tended by a retinue of officials of the service and of coolies in strange hats resembling Halloween. Now the sedan chair was brought into the small courtyard of the house and set down with the bride still in it and the curtains closely drawn. And for half an hour there it sat, while the various officials prepared for the ceremony and the relatives and friends, ably assisted by the strident band, created such confusion and noise as could be equaled nowhere west of Suez. Finally, all was ready (it seems this wait had partly been to test the patience of the bride) and the ceremonies started.

But the confusion did not cease — if anything it grew worse. In-deed it was difficult to distinguish who was taking part in the ceremony and who was part of the cheerful, jabbering, jostling lookers-on.

In the center of the "entrance room" was a table which had on it four great red candles, dishes of fruit and eatables and other things. By this stood the groom's best men (married men and supposed to be wealthy) who were witnesses. By them was the master of ceremonies, a gaunt old fellow whose chief acquisition was a very deep voice. It seems that was why he was the master of ceremonies. He now opened the event by inviting the bride-groom to come to the wedding. The groom was upstairs and the message had to be conveyed up to him. On the third summons he obeyed and came down the creaky stairs. He was placed on a red carpet with his back to the table and the sedan chair. In the meanwhile, the mother of the groom (a hustling old lady) assisted by some other woman relative was feeding the various parties concerned, with a certain kind of soup and food. It seems that this was part of the ceremony of worshiping Heaven.

And now at last they open the sedan chair (it must have been stifling within). She was clad in a beautiful embroidered red robe, but we could see little of it because of a red curtain which enveloped her whole head and fell to her waist. Now she walks (or is rather shoved and pushed) over a carpet of old rice sacks to a place opposite the groom. The rice sacks are significant too. They give happiness of some kind. The master of ceremonies jabbers away, the bride and groom make various bows and motions and steps and this part of the ceremony is over.

The whole party now adjourns upstairs. The bride and groom walking on rice sacks and there amid further confusion the operations are continued in the bridal chamber itself! It seems that they must now worship the bridal bed, and to do so they sit together on the bed, the same old flutes continue their unearthly noise and further ceremonies are conducted.

There is now a breathing spell and the long suffering bride is relieved of her cloth covering. Beneath is a most elaborate headdress of silver and tinsel, and hanging in front of her face so that you can scarcely see her, are strings of beads.

I took this opportunity to leave the scene, as I had study hour in the evening and I left with a feeling of the utter senselessness and tawdriness of the whole ceremony. The groom did not believe in all the trash he was going through — that was evident from his manner — he was simply doing it to please his parents; and the bride could not have either, for she is a Christian. Then too the whole thing was conducted amidst such confusion and terrific noise, and the colors and tinsel of the decorations seem so utterly lacking in our Western ideas of taste, that the whole impression was the most heathenish one I have had in China. Doubtless, however, our own quiet and dignified wedding ceremony would seem just as strange to a Chinese. And now that I think of it, we too have some strange customs at weddings

January, 1917
Sightseeing in Peking

With the advent of China New Year vacation came the long looked for opportunity to visit Peking, and three of us — the two Roberts and myself — resolved to take advantage of it. So on one cold Winter morning an auto summoned us from an early breakfast, and along with three others of the Bachelors who were going up country, we piled in bag and baggage and were twirled to the station. The trip as far as Nanking was no different from our usual ones up country and was through a countryside now very familiar to us: the furrowed fields, the many canals, the conical grave mounds and mud tiled villages and cities. Moreover, the train accommodations were excellent but very little different from a second rate line at home.

At Nanking we disembarked at the ferry station and followed the coolie with our two great bags on board the ferry boat — quite a respectable sized boat resembling a tender on the Whangpoo. The Yangtze at this point, 150 miles from its mouth, is yellow with mud and about half a mile broad, really narrower than I had pictured it from all the accounts of the mighty river. We were interested to see a large percent of the Chinese navy anchored off the city — five small but rather efficient looking gray-colored gunboats. I think I saw some of them at Canton last year. We were interested also in quite another kind of vessel, a beggar boat, which came alongside our ferryboat before we started. Even on the water China has her beggars and they were quite as persistent and as miserable looking as on land. We gave to them in self-defense, placing the coppers in a bag attached to a long pole which they manipulated from their boats below.

Crossing the Yangtze at Nanking: Chinese Navy and Beggar Boats

It was but a few minutes journey across the river and a few steps farther to the station at Prukow where we were to entrain for the north. There were many soldiers about the station as we entered the gate for the train, and they were not the mild looking ones to which we are accustomed in Shanghai, but great bulking brutes in blue padded uniforms with rather brutal faces and long barbaric looking queues. At least this was my first impression of them, though we were to learn later that they were very mild and good natured.

We were scheduled to go Second Class to Peking, with hopes of buying a First Class ticket overnight and a berth. So now we examined the train with much interest. There was a splendid looking English locomotive, followed immediately by two German "Schlafwagens" and a Speisewagen" of rather antique pattern, then came an ancient First Class "chair car," one Second Class car, and five or six Third. Class ones resembling a freight train. It was the Second Class one in which we were particularly interested. From the outside it looked rather rattletrappy, pointless and dirty and we were rather discouraged, but not until we saw the inside did we get the full measure of what was coming to us. There was a long vista of hard looking, high backed wooden benches full to the brim and overflowing with passengers, evil-smelling, dirty-looking, most of them soldiers and all of them so surrounded with their baskets of belongings, their beddings and blankets, their cases and bags, that the car more closely resembled a freight car or a travelling encampment than a respectable vehicle of travel. And it was in this that we were to spend the next two days! Our hearts sank at the entrance, they sank still further when we had entered and searched in vain for an empty compartment, and they sank to our boots when we searched the whole train and found that this was the only Second Class car.

Finally, we decided we must make the best of it. So I found half a seat, Don another, and I plumped my bag down between two Chinese and sat on it. And thus we started our 500-mile journey — no prospect of a seat and surrounded by smells and sights which would have been called disgusting by the fastidious at home. In our car were two other foreigners — a man, evidently a missionary and whom we later found was probably a German, and a young lady who sat off in a corner to herself surrounded by her belongings and effectively blockaded by them. As the train started from Prukow and wound through the great low-lying plain which borders the Yangtze, we struck up an acquaintance almost immediately with our Chinese neighbors. We knew no Mandarin but they were able to understand a little of our Shanghai dialect and with the aid of a little phrase book of Donald's we were soon making ourselves understood. And by the time that evening was over we were talking very readily together and on almost every subject in our immediate neighborhood — the difference in Chinese and foreign customs and dress, how soldiers drill, who was married and who not, why most of the northerners wore queues (it seems that they have to in order to be soldiers), how old we were etc. etc. Once on mention of Japan our particular friend pointed out a very ingratiating little man who sat nearby, told us he was a Jap and then very significantly went through the motions of shooting and of cutting a throat!

By nightfall we were tired of all this prattle and our uncomfortable positions. There would have been plenty of room in the car had it not been for the selfishness of several Chinese. Their belongings sprawled all over the section and left room for only themselves besides. We were cheered up, however, by the news that two of them were to get off at eleven o'clock. We had dinner on the train in the "Spersewagen" and really fared very well. Then we tried to get berths and found everything full up. We were doomed for the night in that evil smelling, closely packed, uncomfortable car! The first part of it was bearable. By the light of tiny little oil lamps, we continued the conversation with our Chinese friends and presently were doing tricks with them. One of them was very clever and did many tricks and stunts with handkerchief, hand and string that we do in the West. But long before midnight (and we did not reach the eleven o'clock station until then) it became terribly monotonous. We finally had to deliberately snub their attentions and there followed a hour or so broken only by the snores of the sleeping multitudes and the hawking spits of those awake. That terrible spitting habit of the Chinese is one of the worst they have. Time, place or occasion matters not to them — they spit when they have to and wherever they happen to be.

Even after our friends left us and we secured the two hard benches to ourselves and our bags, we were far from comfortable. We tried to sleep but the hard benches denied it for more than fifteen minutes at a time. It began to be cold too and we were constantly stopping at stations and being subjected to the uproar of an outgoing and incoming mob. They always met at our end of the car and once there ensued such a scuffle and shouting and shoving as endangered our own long waited for seats. I put my back to the wall and my feet in some Chinese's back and in that way kept them out of our compartment. Down in the middle of the car a quarrel was going on. Outside the flickering oil lights fell on the upturned faces of the mass of pushing locals — it was a scene possessing even more than we wanted of the flavor of the East.

But the night passed, as all bad dreams do, and with the morning came more quiet, more room, a good breakfast, a little heat in the car and much more cheerfulness. We were tired, dirty and longing for exercise but we managed to pass all that day in the same old car with much good cheer. Overnight we were in a new land, what was to us an entirely different China.

Through most of the day we were passing through the great fertile plain of the province of Shantung — but so different from our own Yangtze plain. The soil was dirty yellow, seemingly but dust, there were practically no trees or vegetation of any kind, the villages and cities were clusters of mud huts of the same shade of mud as the land and seeming part of it. We passed over the bed of what was once the Yellow River, and many miles farther on we passed over the present Yellow River — a rather insignificant stream but crossed by a magnificent concrete and iron bridge built by the Germans, and possessing a wide plain for a bed which would have done credit to the largest river in the world. For miles on each side of the river the land was like a billiard table, but farther on this table land rose somewhat and there were sunken roads and gullies and strange formations. This was the loess, or accumulations of hundreds of years of dust. There followed the boundless expanse of yellow, desolate plain, broken only by villages just as yellow and desolate and peopled with fat padded Chinese in blue garments, or by cities surrounded by a wall of mud. At each city was a station, much too magnificent for the low lying, thatched roofed cities. These stations were of various strange architectural conceptions, each purporting to contain something of the Chinese. They were German built and evidently put up for effect. The English built half the line and did it poorly; the Germans outdid themselves in their half.

At nightfall we reached Tientsin, and in the midst of cold which reminds us of New England, we rickshawed to the Imperial Hotel. Seldom have hot water, a shave and a dinner and bed felt better than they did that night.

Much refreshed and ready for a fresh start we awoke on another cold but beautiful day. I called up Mr. Pyke for a few minutes. He used to teach at Yeates and now has charge of the Tientsin Intermediate School. We took a train (Second Class again, but excellent this time) for Peking. E-yah! but it was cold outside. Everything was frozen tight. We were interested in a novel method of getting about over the ice and wondered that it had never been adopted at home. At the rear of a

wide sled a man stood facing the front. Then with a long spiked pole
he proceeded to push the sled forward rapidly over the ice. The pole
was held by both hands and pushed between his legs.

Railway Station Outside Tartar Wall

Across the desolate plain, which they say extends to far off Mongolia, we approached the great [city] walls of Peking. We skirted the outer
wall for a while, darted through it, wound about within this outer wall for
several miles, reached the second or Tartar wall much larger and more
impressive, and finally drew up at the station directly under one of the im-
posing gateways. Then we passed through one of the smaller gateways,
the Water Gate, and proceeded by rickshaw through the city to the third
wall, the great yellow crowned one which guards the Imperial Domain.

Immediately I saw Peking, a phrase came into my mind which as I
found later had been applied to our own Washington. It was "The City
of Magnificent Distances." After seeing more of the city I thought
the phrase a most apt one. It is a city of distances. There is a breadth
and a freedom about it which is inspiring and which might truly be
called magnificent. That afternoon, when we had finished tiffin at the
Hotel de Peking and had gotten in communication with friends (Don-

* During the Cultural Revolution, Chairan Mao had these magnificent walls of the
city torn down.

51

ald Caruthers, and a friend of his, Jack Lyons) they began to show us about and we began to appreciate the greatness of the city. We walked on the Tartar wall, a tremendous piece of work with a top wide enough for four teams to drive abreast, and from its commanding height looked upon the city. If we had had time we could have walked completely around the wall — 16 miles! As it was we could only see the Legation Quarter. It lay just below us as we walked; British, Dutch, German, American, Japanese, each compound with its distinctive type of architecture and the whole an impressive International display. Over the beautiful American buildings, the flag floated at half-mast because of [Admiral] Dewey's death, on the great wall above the Legation was a huge wireless mast (which had probably brought news of his death), and along the wall strode a big American sentry with his Springfield [rifle] over his shoulder and his great coat and fur hat for this northern climate. It was splendid to see it all.

A little further on we came to the great entrance gate of the city which led in turn to another huge gate of red with green tilings for a roof, and that in turn by a huge far-reaching courtyard to another and yet more splendid yellow tiled gate, until far in the distance could be seen the yellow tiled roofs of the Imperial city. Truly it was an impressive entrance to a wonderful Empire; an entrance which by its simplicity and "magnificent distances" would do justice to the capital of any country in the world.

That night we had dinner and became established at the Stuart's home on the Methodist Mission Compound, a very fine place built of Boxer Indemnity money. We hope to save money by thus living in a private home.

The next day, cold and clear as seems to be the custom up here, was one of the most perfect sightseeing ones I have ever experienced. After a long rickshaw ride down wide Hatamen Street with its low Chinese shops and houses, its tremendous traffic of rickshaws, pedestrians, donkeys, Peking carts, horses, automobiles and long strings of camels, and its distinctly Oriental air, we reached the Presbyterian Mission and "La's" friend Jack Lyons home. Then with him as a most efficient guide we started on our sightseeing.

Temple of Confucius

The wonderful Temple of Confucius, in itself of the utmost and most solemn grandeur, has a setting well in accord with its magnificence. The wide outer courtyard is thickly studded with pines and the sun shines dimly through and lights up in patches the tablets erected to those who have passed the third and highest examination in the past seven centuries. Then a splendid gateway which contains stone drums more than 2500 years old leads to an inner courtyard even finer than the first. Here too are pines and through them leads a stone passageway to the steps of the Temple itself. As we passed along we could hear a strange rich whistling sound overhead, a flock of pigeons with whistles tied to their tails. And the interior of the Temple in its solemnity and expanse and grandeur surpasses anything I have yet seen. The whole building has recently been redecorated in preparation for Yuan Shi-kai's resumption of the Imperial Throne and so we had the opportunity of seeing it as it originally was a most unusual thing in China. In the vast rectangular hall, huge red pailows rose to a great height and supported a richly decorated roof in violet and blue and gold. At one end of the great hall was a simple but magnificent shrine containing a small red tablet with the characters "The tablet of the soul of the most holy ancestral teacher, Confucius" and on other sides similar tablets to Tseng-tsze, Mencius, Yen hui, Tszu-szu — and that was all. It was the simplicity and dignity and good taste, and the vastness and dimness of the temple which gave it its magnificence.

View from the Drum Tower

Back of the Temple is the Hall of the Classics, where the Emperor used to sit and have the Holy Books read to him, and surrounding the Hall, in order that the Classics might never be forgotten, they are inscribed on tablets of stone. Back still further is a magnificent pailow of stone richly decorated.

From here we went to the great Drum Tower, where a soldier showed us up a steep stairway of immense stone steps and from which we had a wide view of the whole of Peking. It lay out before us like a map, with its Chinese wall far in the distance, the great Tartar Wall with the four huge gates within, the Imperial City wall within that and the multitudinous yellow tiled roofs of the Forbidden City in the very center. Nearby was the bell tower, the wide streets with their crowded traffic and gray tiled Chinese houses and courtyards, interspersed with trees.

We had tiffin with Lyons in his Chinese house; a Chinese tiffin of rice and various meats and a great charcoal brazier in the center of the table full of luscious ham and meat balls called "*hau chub kuk mehz.*" And in the afternoon we saw a Buddhist Idol in process of erection, being beaten out slowly of brass, and thence to the Temple. Here there are about 1500 Lama priests (dirty looking fellows in red shawl-like robes) who continue the services started by the Emperor Yung Ching. Also there are many small boys who act as acolytes. They are presented to the Temple at birth.

The Making of an Idol

The Temple itself is yellow tiled and magnificent but falling into decay. There is a splendid approach with a fine pailows, a very fine courtyard with four small pagodas and many old trees, a huge entrance pavilion, an inner courtyard with a great tablet telling in four languages — Tibetan, Mongol, Chinese and Manchu — of the history of Lamaism, many small worship rooms, the Temple itself, and in the rear a huge building containing a hideous but impressive statue of Buddha seventy-feet high!

But what was to me the most interesting thing about the Temple was the service which we had the good fortune to see. In a small side worship room or chapel, richly decorated and crowded with a great table bearing candles and incense burners and strange vessels and fruits, sat two lines of yellow clad priests and boys on the floor. At their head and before a small table sat the head priest or lama — a fat, wrinkled old man in yellow robes and huge horn spectacles. The priests were chanting in guttural tones the reading of the holy books and occasionally they would stop, whereupon the old man would ring a bell and rattle an odd instrument; then the flood of harsh, reading would continue.

The effect of the whole scene was nearest to what our imagination pictures heathen rites of anything I have seen in the East. The dimness of the room full of shaven priests and strange instruments of worship, the heavy candle smoke, the old lama, the guttural singsong, gave an impression I shall never forget. And presently it became even more heathenish, for at a signal from the old lama there broke forth music more outlandish than anything Barnum and Bailey or the Hippodrome ever tried to imitate. Strange twisted horns shrieked, great drums shaped like child's rattle boomed, and two horns at least fifteen feet long gave forth great bass sounds. Then there came forward two richly dressed Chinese, who kowtowed three times and were blessed by the old lama.

We now went by rickshaw outside the city walls and across a windswept, beggar infested desolate plain to another Lama Temple, the Yellow Temple, where the Grand Lama is supposed to reside when he visits Peking. He is at present in Tibet, being only eleven years old. Each succeeding Lama is selected by electing the baby who was born the instant the old Lama died. In the Yellow Temple the chief thing of interest is an exquisite marble monument to a Lama who died of smallpox while on a visit here. On it is depicted in carvings the story of his life.

When the "Allies" held Peking after the Boxer trouble, some French troops were quartered in the Temple and it is reported used the carvings as targets in mere wanton destruction. Certainly the face of practically every figure is gone. Nor is this the only instance of vandalism by the foreigner during Boxer times still to be seen in Peking.

January 23, 1917

Peking residents are certainly fortunate as to weather. This day, China New Year, again dawned bright and clear with briskness in the air which made our blood tingle. When we first arrived we felt the cold pretty severely on our faces, toes, and fingers, but now we have become somewhat accustomed to it. In the morning, along with a party from the Presbyterian Mission (Jack Lyons, Mr. and Mrs. Smith, Dr. Wiley and Dr. Dietrich, who has been in China but two months after two years on the Austro-German front) we passed by rickshaw through streets gay with New Year decorations, outside the Tartar wall and to the enclosure of The Temple and Altar of Heaven.

It was here that the Emperors used to worship Heaven once a year, not Confucius or Buddha or any god, but Heaven itself. The Altar is approached by a long stone avenue lined with pines. At the end of this entrance drive is a large building called the Hall of Abstinence where the Emperor prepared by a night of fasting and prayer for the worship on the morrow. Then the avenue led on through several gates to the Altar itself. It is of marble, much whitewashed now, built in three tiers, each of which is mounted by nine steps, each tier surrounded by beautiful posts and balustrades of a type much in evidence in the Imperial part of Peking. The whole structure has great simplicity and dignity and when seen against the green of the surrounding pines, with the deep blue of the low enclosing wall to add one other touch of color, it is magnificent. Nearby is a great incense furnace and many incense pots and just outside the wall, a stone platform for the Emperor's pavilion under which a great fire can be kindled.

The Altar of Heaven

The round block of marble in the center of the Altar of Heaven is supposed by the Chinese to be the center of the Universe. From it lead the four entrances to the Altar and down one of these, through an archway of pailows and past a smaller wall-enclosed Temple is the splendid Temple of Heaven. It is on a foundation which resembles the Altar, and the Temple itself is a round building richly decorated and surmounted by a three-tiered roof of deep blue and crowned by a knob or "button" of gold gilt.

Courtyard and Entrance Gateway to Throne Room

After tiffin (at the Stuarts) we visited that part of Peking which represents the center of the Chinese Empire, the Imperial City. We paid 10 cents to pass through the beautiful entrance gateway to what is called Central Park. There was little of interest there and we walked through it until we came to a huge moat and another wall, the Forbidden City. Fifteen cents let us in here and we passed through yet another huge gate and into the outer courtyard of the Court of China. It was truly magnificent. A great wide expanse of white pavement intersected by a winding stream with marble bridges, impressive flights of stone steps, richly decorated entrance gates, great bronze lions guarding the inner entrance, and over it all and in splendid color contrast, the Imperial yellow of the curved porcelain tiled roofs. Through the inner

58

gateway, guarded (as were all the gates) by fine looking soldiers and officers, was the courtyard of the City, very similar to the outer, but having at its northern end the Throne Room of the Empire. The interior of this reminded one of the Temple of Confucius; it was huge, simple and dignified, its only article of furniture the elaborate dais, throne, and screen.

Back of the Throne Room was another courtyard and another smaller Throne Room, we supposed for private audiences, and back of that could be seen the roofs of the only part of the Forbidden City not accessible, the present home of the young "would be" Emperor and the deposed Imperial Manchu family.

Before leaving the Imperial City we visited the Imperial Museum, passing hurriedly by its priceless treasures of cloisonné, gold, jade, embroideries and pottery. In it one speaks in centuries instead of years and the contents can scarcely be measured in terms of money. I have never had a higher opinion of the wonderful ability of the Chinese artisans, of the taste and culture of the race, or indeed of the ability of mankind as a whole to express beauty in inanimate objects than on witnessing this great collection of Chinese treasures.

We completed our day by climbing the huge Buddhist "dagoba," with its strange inverted bell shape. From it could be seen most of the Imperial City and directly below lay the chain of three lakes. On islands in these lakes were the residences of the current President of China — Li Yuan-hung, and far in the distance we could see the tall flag staff bearing the five bared flag of the Republican China and a crow's nest which they say is never empty of a watchful sentinel. Back of the dagoba is the former residence of Yuan 's son, bordered by a lake with temples and pailows on its further side. There was about two feet of ice on this "Bei ho" or North Lake, and in spite of our soldier guide's warnings of danger, we crossed it. We found the ruins of what had once been a series of magnificent Temples, and many interesting statues, shrines etc. We brought away relics — I have the plaster hand of a neglected and decrepit Buddhist idol.

President Li Yuan-hung and Staff

January 25, 1917

There now followed two days somewhat devoid of active sight-seeing but none the less interesting. We wandered about the Peking streets, did a little shopping for Chinese lanterns and cloisonné, called on friends and had dinner at several places. One afternoon Donald and I called on Mrs. Ragland, wife of the athletic director of the Y.M.C.A. and found her charming. We had dinner there the next evening — Chinese chow and the best yet. Another time we tried skating at the American rink. It was "Central Powers" day and it was interesting to watch the German and Austrian Embassy elite on the ice. They skate beautifully. Peking abounds in skating rinks and seems to be the chief amusement of society. There is music and dancing on the ice. Still another time we visited the American Legation on "at home" day, met the Minister and Mrs. Reinsch, a few other notables, some pretty girls and had some fine dances in the ball room.

One night there was a musicale on the Methodist Compound which was most enjoyable. And another evening we had dinner at the Krauses where I found that Mrs. Krause was from Princess Anne, Maryland. Also we had tea at the Anglican Mission with Bishop Norris and Mr. Denham-Brown. The Bishop is most entertaining, given perhaps to rather extreme and unusual statements, but then you see that he is really joking.

The only real sightseeing we did was the Summer Palace. There was a St. John's man (Mr. Chao) in Peking who, among other business activities, owned the Peking garage. He invited us to go to the Summer Palace with him in one of his cars. So, along with another St. John's man, a Mr. Lok of the Police Department and his wife and a friend, (all of whom spoke Shanghai dialect by the way) we set out in two cars. Ours, a Chalmers, came to grief from tire trouble, and the big "American" which we then entered broke down just under one of the big gates of the Tartar wall. So while waiting for the Chalmers to come again, we went through the nearby Zoological Gardens and had Chinese tiffin.

Camels Outside the Wall

In the afternoon we finally got off and travelled down a very good stone road to the Palace. The road was modern in the center, Chinese made on the both sides, with great stone slabs, and lined with trees. It was most interesting and full of traffic: donkeys, Peking carts, rickshaws and occasional trains of camels. It swarmed with soldiers, as there are huge barracks near the palace. For that matter all Peking is full of soldiers; they say about 30,000 in all. They are of many different kinds: blue clad with white caps who act as police, yellow clad with great coats and yellow caps and leggings who seem to be the regulars but also help in policing, and grey clad ones which we could not classify.

JAM at Summer Palace

We found the Summer Palace well worth all our misadventures in reaching it. There was a beautiful lake, rich pagodas, many fine pailows, a splendid marble bridge, and on a hill at one end of the lake the palace; itself a succession of yellow tiled gateways one above another and leading up the hillside to a huge pagoda flanked by many other buildings and smaller pagodas, one of which was of solid bronze. The rear of the hill consisted of very fine half wild gardens, containing the ruins of a temple which reminded one in its architecture of Nineveh and Tyre.

On the way home from the Palace we drove through Tseng Hua College. It has very nice grounds and a large handsome grey and white stone modern college building. Then we passed the entrance to the old Summer palace, down an old Chinese road of huge badly-fitting stone slabs, on to the modern road, and there to Peking again.

January 27, 1917

This last day of our Peking visit we reserved for a trip to the Great Wall of China — one of the wonders of the world, which I suppose every school-boy longs to see — at least I know I did. We had invited the Stuarts — Mr. and Mrs. and his sister — to go with us, and after an early breakfast the six of us started out in rickshaws. We had to cross the whole Tartar city and it was a long, cold ride in the misty early morning before we reached the station.

The Great Wall at Nankou Pass

It used to be that a trip to the Great Wall was an undertaking only for the hardened traveler, for Peking carts and donkeys or camels were the only means of conveyance; but now there is a very good railroad with American locomotives, and you are whirled across the great flat plain surrounding the city, and hauled up the steep winding gradient into the mountains without inconvenience and almost, indeed, in comfort.

We reached the famous Nankou Pass through which the caravan trains from Mongolia enter the plain to Peking, passed through and on into the rocky and mountainous country beyond, until we reached a little station deep in a cleft of the hills. There we disembarked (having eaten picnic tiffin on the train) and walked up thru a valley. And at its head was a path leading through a double gateway, and the famous

Wall stretched away and up on both sides as far as the eye could reach.

We climbed by an inclined plane onto its top and walked along its winding and precipitous length. The wall was about thirty feet high and fifteen wide. The base was of granite blocks, the top of sun dried bricks. On the Mongolian side were battlements and loopholes, but towards China the escarpment was solid and not as high. Every 300 yards or so along the wall was a tower, much higher and bigger than the wall itself and so placed as to enable the defenders to shoot along its length down upon the attacking Mongols. But it was not these dimensions of the wall which made it so impressive, for there are many walls in China much larger, but it was the realization of its tremendous 1500-mile length and the view which we could get of a few miles of that length from the top of one of the high peaks bordering the pass. From this height the Wall lay stretched out before us like a great snake, hugging close every contour of the very mountainous district over which it passed. Just below us it dipped down over the mountain side until its top was almost perpendicular and steps were necessary in order that it might be climbed, on the other side of the pass it rose just as precipitously, and far off in the distance we could see it outlined against the sky on a ridge or clinging to the side of a rocky slope. And when we realized that it did this for 1500 miles, we knew that it was properly named "The Great Wall."

We took many pictures of the wall, ate the remainder of our tiffin, addressed postcards home while sitting on its top, watched the caravans of laden donkeys pass through the two gateways (the outer at the wall and the inner at the screen), and finally had to leave to make our train for Peking.

That night we packed our bags and said our final goodbyes — with great regret. Peking is one of the few places which fully lives up to all one hears about it.

The Great Wall

The Great Wall at Nankou Pass

The Great Wall at Nankou Pass

January 29, 1917

All that afternoon and night we were on the train in a compartment of our own and with a large central room to ourselves, so we were very comfortable. There was only one other First Class foreign passenger, a young fellow named Saunders, B.A.T., just out. I had an interesting talk with him about his work. The next morning just after breakfast in the "Restaurant" car, our train came to a halt in the open country and the Chinese passengers began to disembark with all their luggage. We found that there was a wreck ahead. Some weeks before a troop train had gone through the first section of a tall slender bridge spanning the almost dry bed of a river which we later found was the Hu. There were hundreds of coolies and a few French engineers busy repairing things, but the bridge was still down, the cars lay at the bottom of the deep ravine, and things were in a terrible mess. We heard that eleven men had lost their lives in the wreck. We had to walk over an improvised causeway of sleepers across the shallow river and take another train waiting there.

*Wrecked Bridge Over Hu River**

All that day we traveled southward through a country constantly growing more like Shanghai and hence, more familiar. Graves, water

* see End Notes

66

buffalo, and rice fields put in their appearance; there were occasional hills, the villages again had mud tiled roofs, and the country itself lost its desolate appearance and there was even a semblance of green in the fields. It was constantly growing warmer too and the people were not as thickly padded as farther north.

When we arrived at Hankow at 6 o'clock we were in a quandary as to where to go or what to do. Our train was late, no one met us, we did not know at which of the three stations to disembark, we knew practically no Mandarin and the Chinese officials spoke only French. Finally, we got off at the first station, took rickshaws and said "Sung Kung whei." And after a short ride through Hankow's wide streets which to us (after the cold of the north) smelt of Spring and were strangely silent and attractive, we landed up at the very place they were expecting us for the night, Mr. Littell's.

Mr. Littell was a Trinity man, and his wife used to be at school with my sisters and knew lots of people that I did (as did he too) so my stay there was delightful. They have a splendidly furnished home and three attractive children.

Hankow, Wuchang and Hanyang are three cities at the branches of the Han and Yangtze Rivers. Hankow is a beautiful foreign city with British, Russian, French, German, and Japanese Concessions located on a beautiful Bund on the Yangtze; Hanyang is a manufacturing place — being the location of the great Hanyang Ironworks and a Government Arsenal; and Wuchang is a Chinese walled city where the Revolution started in 1911[*]. We were in the former two of these cities for about two days and saw everything that was possible in that time. We heard while in, of a great earthquake which occurred while we were in Peking. Nearly all China felt it, and at Hanchow it was quite severe. Formosa is reported to have been the center.

On Jan. 31[st.] we crossed the Yangtze by sampan and boarded the *Kiang Wu* of China Merchant's Line for our trip down the river. She was a very comfortable, side-wheeled, vivid yellow ship, reminding me very much of the dear old steamers which cross our own Chesapeake. The river was unusually shallow because of the dry weather. It was 46 ft. lower than in Summer time and our Captain was afraid we would go aground. As we passed the shallow places four men were kept busy

[*] known as the Xinhai Revolution, it eventually overthrew the Qing Dynasty

throwing the lead and calling out the depth. Our ship drew 8'4" of water and once we passed a spot only 8 ft. deep, so it was ticklish going. After dinner (they gave us excellent chow) we anchored for the night and the next morning were held in the same spot until 12 o'clock by a heavy fog. This delayed our arrival at Anking (we stopped at Kiukiang enroute and saw something of the city) and it was after 12 at night when we finally got off the hulk, jammed with its excited Chinese, and walked up through the narrow hilly streets to our Mission Compound.

I spent the night with Jim Pott in his rooms in the school building (Mahan School) and the Roberts were at the Lee's. The next day we had an all day's walking trip to the mountains which are within view from the river. From the top there was a magnificent view of the Yangtze Valley.

The next night we caught another river steamer and started on our last lap home. When the boat stopped at Chinkiang we got an evening paper with the astonishing news of America's severing diplomatic relations with Germany and the prospect of war. But the world kept on moving and we arrived safely at St. John's the next day.

July 1917
To Tientsin and Chili Mountains

天津

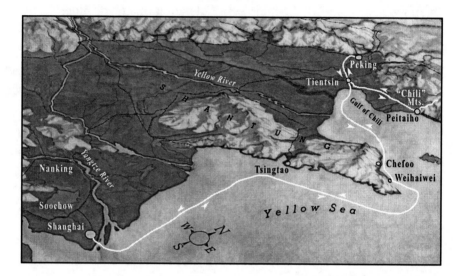

The last week of June 1917, the last week of our college year also, was almost unbearably hot. All the pent-up heat and humidity of a cool Spring seemed concentrated and to be loosing itself upon Shanghai. You awoke in the morning soaked with perspiration, panting under your mosquito net, and listless in every muscle and joint. While you shaved with one hand and slapped at mosquitoes with the other, your boy brought a bucket of water to reinforce the reluctant shower. This gave energy enough to dress and then, accoutered in white and a topee, you braved the heat to reach the Mess for breakfast. The heat struck you like a wave as you passed outside. The sun hung in a blue sky; masses of white chiseled clouds bordered the horizon; the world below shimmered in the heat.

The breakfast room was rendered bearable by a punka, lazily pulled by a half-naked coolie. Under it, you viewed with disgust the offerings for breakfast. You tried to eat mushy shredded wheat and watery milk and failed; revolted at the sound of hot eggs, and pushed aside the hot coffee and hotter bread. You finally breakfasted on a banana and a glass of water.

Then followed the day's work; a day of ordeal, sweltering in the closeness, perspiring constantly. Tiffin brought only the relief of the punka; it did not mean nourishment, for you were unable to get food down.

The heat reached its climax about two or three, when the whole world was like a great hot box with the lid tightly closed. No relief seemed possible. You panted like an animal and moved about aimlessly, searching for air. At four you again sought the punka and tried the traditional Chinese cooling drink — hot tea. Around six it had cooled off somewhat and you ventured a set of tennis. One set was quite enough.

Dinner was a meal only in that you were able to consume a large quantity of so called ice cream. The evening was fairly comfortable so long as one was in the open air and clear of the trees. There was a moon that week, when it was not obscured by the low lying heat clouds, and under it most of the Compound was accustomed to wander about, or sit quietly. We all sat late, for it was useless to go to bed. I was up some nights until long after twelve.

But eventually we all did wander back to our beds, braving the mosquitoes and the thousand and one varieties of horrible bugs of China. Once under the net and having completed the fight with the mosquitoes who got in with you, you were still lucky if you could sleep. Most of the night consisted of twisting and squirming and perspiring. And with the morning would come another day of heat.

It was in the midst of this that we lived for the last week of college, that we corrected our examination papers, made up our marks, attended meetings, made trips to town, and finally witnessed Class Day and the 21st Commencement of the University.

While we were in the midst of this and living our daily lives peacefully, if not comfortably, China was in convulsion politically. A month before, the old regime under President Li had come to a crisis over the question of the war with Germany. At least this question was an excuse under which political ambition and greed were working to allow each individual to fill his own pockets and his own vanity. It came to a head with the dismissal of Parliament by the assembled Tuchuns, or warlords, in Peking and the threat of civil war through the Republic. Then the great bandit leader, Chang Hsun, the Tuchun of Shantung, went to Peking in person to act as mediator. He carried with him a picked bodyguard of 5,000 troops and with them proceeded to terrorize the capital. On July 2nd. came the astonishing news that the Monarchy had been reestablished, the young Manchu Emperor had been put on the throne; China was again an Empire. Chang Hsun was of course back of the move. He was the "real" Emperor.

Under these conditions we left for the Summer.

I had planned for a vacation in the north on the seashore, and was to go up by sea. At the last minute Miss Bates, of St. Mary's, was obliged to give up her plans of travelling by rail and was able to get passage on the same boat. We sailed on the third of July, on the afternoon of one of the hottest of Shanghai's hot days. The ship was the *Koonshing*, a British boat, fairly large and comfortable, with accommodations for about twenty-five or thirty First Class passengers. There were about that number on board, most of them being children.

MV Koonshing

It was good to get away from the steaming caldron of the Shanghai! As we crept down the muddy Whangpoo with its low lying green banks and slowly out into the even muddier mouth of the great Yangtze, I felt that a burden was being pulled off my back. It was but little cooler on the Yangtze but there was at least space to breathe and the open sea was ahead of us.

71

Britishers are not very communicative and our shipmates were chiefly British, so it was a day or so before we began to know them. They were chiefly women going north for the Summer, and each woman had her allotment of children in tow. We never did completely straighten out which children belonged to which mother. Also there were a few British men — Mr. Kemp of the Public Schools in Shanghai, a Canadian, Mr. Crawley of the government at Weihaiwei. And among the women were two colorless English girls.

But by far the most interesting man on board excepting the Captain who was a thorough gentleman, was a French soldier who had just returned from the front because of wounds. He was my cabin mate so I got to know him pretty well and he had not the slightest objection to talking of his experiences. He was typically French in appearance; expressive eyes, mustache, and clothes, and he lived up to their reputation also in his talkativeness, and gaiety. He played the violin and tooted a big brass horn and helped amuse the whole ship with both. Also he had a most interesting looking Toochin "boy" with him, a quite small fellow with great baggy trousers and a black half turban who spoke only French.

JAM with French Travelling Companion

72

"Our Frenchman," as we called him, had been wounded in the Battle of the Somme. He had received two bullets in the stomach and was left in the German first line trenches when his comrades retreated after a charge. He regained consciousness to find himself surrounded by enemies, found he could move, and immediately started to crawl away towards his own line.

The Germans saw him and began to throw hand grenades. One fell within his reach, so he picked it up and threw it back! It fell in their midst and exploded, disconcerting them so much that he was able to crawl out of their reach. Then they began to fire at him with rifles. One bullet struck his clothes. But he reached the French trench and tumbled in. That was his own tale, and he had many others as interesting to relate.

We had a quiet trip up the China Coast. After the first night, which was very hot and close, a fine breeze sprang up and for two days we almost shivered in it. It was delightful to be cool again.

At Weihaiwei we dropped many of our passengers. It is a British Concession, granted at the same time Germany obtained Tsingtao. A beautiful little island dotted with recently planted trees stands near the mainland. On it are a few cottages and houses, and over its hills is laid a golf course. The larger part of the town is on the mainland, the chief building being a large hotel. But the whole place is rather insignificant. It is merely a strategic base and loses money for Britain yearly.

Coastline Near Chefoo

A few hours sail down a beautiful rock strewn, hill bounded coast, which in places resembled the Inland Sea of Japan and in places the coast of Lower California, brought us to the port of Chefoo. This is an International Settlement and also something of a Summer resort. Its harbor is very beautiful. A rocky point crowned with a brilliantly white lighthouse, juts out into the sea and divides the shipping portion from the residence section most conveniently. The houses are scattered along a long curve of the beach. To be sure the water looked dirty and not very inviting, but the general situation was splendid. On the rear of the town rose a huge bare hill, along the summit of which crawls an absurd Chinese Wall about six feet in height, built so they say, to keep the Tartars out!

Those of us who were left on the boat — our Frenchman, the two English girls, Miss Bates and myself — took rickshaws through the town. We wandered through the business portion with its ancient buildings and touch of Europe in its atmosphere, down the beach on the so called "Bund" which was dead to the world on this hot afternoon, and then up the hill and in and out among various cottages and vineyards and Chinese houses. The most conspicuous building was that of a great school for boys and girls. It was in session during the Summer; their long vacation comes at Christmas. We ended up our rickshaw trip by passing through a large Chinese town situated on the hillside. It was a typical city of the northern type. The houses were of brick, fairly well preserved and seemingly very clean after our Yangtze valley hovels. The streets too seemed fairly clean except that they were populated by the usual assembly of dirty children and men and women and beggars and dogs. I mention the children first because they were cleanest, most of them being destitute of clothes and hence having less space to carry dirt. At one place a circus was going on; a huge crowd sat in a sort of amphitheatre in the hillside, and from a stage of bamboo poles and matting there issued the discordant notes of a Chinese band.

As our ship left Chefoo harbor that night, we were treated to a magnificent sight. Lights twinkled along the long curve of the shore, the lighthouse on the hill sent out its flashings of red, another buoy light flashed white, and overhead a wonderful moon made a pathway of brilliance across the quiet water through which there crept now and then the square sail of a Chinese junk. And to make it all complete our Frenchman played fitting solos on the violin.

There were two interesting events on our sea voyage. On the rocky coast a ship had gone ashore. We could see only her funnel and masts above the water and they lay at a great angle, as though the ship were ready at any time to slip off into deep water. She was the *Anping*, a China Merchants ship, and had gone ashore in a fog. Then one day about noontime as we were all lazily reading on deck, and the ship was going steadily ahead on a very quiet sea, there came a sudden ringing of the engine room bells and the ship began suddenly to make a great curve to the right. We looked at the sea and there floated by a life preserver — nothing more was to be seen. The ship made a great circle and a boat was let down, but all it could do was to search aimlessly and pick up the life preserver. A Chinese passenger, one of the many coolies we had taken on at Weihaiwei who were returning to their homes after being rejected for work in Europe, had jumped overboard. He was never seen after he struck the water.

We arrived at the mouth of the coffee colored river up which Tientsin is located in the middle afternoon. It was hot again, and as we wound up the narrow stream, a land breeze blew across the flat country, bringing with it all the accumulated heat of the day. Near the mouth of the stream there was a large town stretching far along its length. It was of the type which one finds throughout the great Manchurian plain, a city seemingly indigenous with the soil. The smooth clay baked walls of the buildings were of exactly the same shade of yellow as the clay soil; the roofs of smooth packed rushes were of like tint; and the very river seemed of the same yellowish hue. Naked children played on the banks, some few swam in the yellow flood; half naked coolies could be seen up the narrow streets going about their business, others came to the river for buckets of water, still others sat in the shade and talked. The whole scene was essentially uncivilized; it made one think more of Africa than China.

Up the river we came to fields of rice and other grains, and here there was the interesting spectacle of the ancient Egyptian style of raising water by means of sweeps. The fields directly adjoined the river which at this point flowed between perpendicular banks of yellow clay.

A coolie stood on the board overhanging the stream and worked the bucket up and down, emptying the water directly into the ditch which flooded the rice fields. A simple but most effective system.

Another interesting sight was the great sinks for extracting salt. Power for pumping the water was obtained by a circular frame containing about six or eight square sails, which went merrily around in a circle.

A little further on the flat countryside became somewhat wooded, and soon we were winding through a region thickly dotted with small trees and shrubs, and interspersed with fields of rice, and more little yellow villages.

We reached Tientsin at nightfall after a journey of about forty miles up the narrow stream. We passed streets which reminded me of a city at home, say Philadelphia, and which seemed most out of place after the country we had been witnessing all afternoon. The docks were noisy and smelly and crowded with merchandise, as are docks all over the world.

That evening Miss Bates and I went out in search of amusement. We rickshawed through the silent streets, trying to keep track of our path as we looked for the nearest hotel. It gives one the feeling of real adventure to wander thus in rickshaws at nighttime through a strange city. We found the hotel and a newspaper. Startling news! Peking was cut off from Tientsin; fighting was going on the railroad line! The bandit Tuchun, Chang Hsun, who had brought about the situation I described earlier in this account and who was really the head of the new Manchu regime, was finding opposition in carrying out his plans. Most of the northern generals had declared against him; the whole country to the south had revolted en masse. He was master only of Peking. And now the Army of the Republic was driving Chang's pig-tail army back up the railroad toward Peking with the intention of driving him out of the city also. Chang was tearing up the railway as he fell back. This was contrary to the Protocol signed with the foreign powers after the Boxer Trouble. According to this Protocol, the railroad was to be kept clear. So the legations had protested, and a force of International troops had been dispatched that morning from Tientsin to go through to Peking and protect the legations. They had gotten to Fengtai and there, were held up by Chang Hsun's troops who had torn up the road and furthermore threatened to fire on the train.[*]

This was the situation when we reached Tientsin, but notwithstanding the fact that fighting was going on within a few miles, the city showed no signs of excitement. Foreigners always look lightly upon Chinese revolutions. Miss Bates and I went to a Cinema show that evening and enjoyed a number of war films and one of Charlie Chaplin. Afterwards we had great difficulty in finding our ship, but finally did so and passed a very uncomfortable night because of the heat and the noise of the coolies. Chinese seem to talk all night long on hot nights.

The next morning, we did some shopping and I made the discovery that the money which I had brought north with me consisted entirely of "Bank of China" notes and they were worth about 60 cents on the dollar! Furthermore, the Tientsin branch of the Hong Kong and Shanghai Bank refused to take them off my hands, though it had been that bank in Shanghai which gave them to me.

After our shopping came the task of getting our baggage from the ship to the railroad station. It is not easy to travel in a region where you do not know the dialect. But I finally obtained a cart and then we had a procession to the station, cart in front, closely followed by Bates and self in rickshaws, guarding it. Then there came Customs, and weighing of baggage, and paying for overweight, and countless hands stuck out for money, and countless voices speaking the guttural vowels of this northern lingo. But we finally found ourselves on the platform awaiting the train. And we waited and waited. Our Frenchman came down in all the glory of a new Winter uniform and regaled us with more stories and gaiety, but the train did not come. And it never did come! We heard later that it was held up by the troops of Chang Hsun, and fired on. The passengers had to lie down on their stomachs for safety; the engineer deserted, and a foreigner finally ran the train through safely to Tientsin.

But they gave us another train finally, and we started off an hour and a half late for Peitaiho. Opposite us sat a party of Germans, in fact the whole train abounded in them. So I read an account of the battle of Verdun (in *Atlantic Monthly*) with our friends, the enemy, just opposite me. It was a hot, uneventful trip and we reached the station at Peitaiho safely in the midst of a welcoming shower.

* see End Notes

August 1917
On Donkeys Through Chili Mountains.

Setting Out on Donkey Back

One of the things to do in Peitaiho is a long walking and donkey trip to the mountains. The mountains can be seen on clear days standing out on the horizon in varying shades of blue, very cool looking and inviting. Among their saw-teeth there is a conspicuous one of rounded hump. This is known as the "Pei-nyui-ting" or the "mountain which backs the cow" and was the object of our particular pilgrimage.

We were a party of ten: two young married ladies, Mrs. Hoagland and Jordan; four men, Mr. Lattimore and his brother, known to us all as Uncle Aleck, Stanard and myself; and two other Lattimore children, Dickie and Eleanore. For this party we had seven riding donkeys, about seven pack donkeys and mules, and a "donkey boy" for each animal.

A donkey at all times is a fearful and wonderful beast, and when in combination with a Chinese "donkey-boy" of even less intelligence he merits some consideration. To begin with he is hardy, made so by hard treatment and heavy blows from his cruel master, and to end with, he is stupid. Between these two he can be anything — stubborn, spiteful, patient, cranky, vicious or playful. He sometimes objects to wetting his

78

feet at a mountain stream; sometimes to climbing rocks. At any hour of the day and night he is apt to become suddenly melodious and make the mountains ring with his hideous bray. And in case he does so, every other donkey must answer him and every donkey boy smile inanely as though his beast had the sweetest voice. At such times no amount of beating can suppress the noise. The donkey is supposedly guided by dirty reins held in the hands of the rider, but he is really controlled by his master, who walks behind him and yells certain words which make him go forward, backward, to the right, left etc., etc. Their sounds are reinforced by persuasive blows from the whip and hand. Some of the words sound thus: To the right — "*Wo-wo-wo.*" Left — "*Yui-yui-yui.*" Stop — "*Yuih h-h.*" Also there is a certain "*Pr-r-r-oo-t,*" (go quickly) which resembles closely the magic word used by Stevenson to make his French donkey, Modestine, move on.

Rest Stop on Way to Chili Mountains

So it was on such beasts as these that our party was relying for the long flat stretches and to carry our bedding and food. This bedding consisted of folding camp cots and a blanket apiece and the food of such canned goods as baked beans, sardines, sausage, butter, coffee, cocoa, milk, hominy, olives etc., etc. There were pots and pans and patent stoves and one big basket of long bottles with which to wash it all down.

Thus equipped, we gathered early one hot morning to start the trip. The girls appeared in such boyish clothes as Army campaign hats, men's shirts and various combinations of riding trousers and "shorts." Mrs. Jordan alone had on dresses and the first forenoon she fell in a bog up to her knees and thenceforth appeared in more sensible bloomers and "middy." The men were in white or khaki and wore sun helmets.

After much haggling with the donkey men; the dismissal of such donkeys as looked too flea bitten; much jabbering in the process of packing; we were finally off. Down the village street, past the last foreign cottage, out in the open shore of the Gulf. Most of the morning we went down the coast, past such things as sand dunes, dead jelly fishes, savage looking nomadic Chinese huts, fishermen in various stages of undress pulling in nets to a barbaric chant. Then we cut inland, passed the last trace of foreign civilization in the shape of a railroad, had something to drink in a pretty little valley with real trees, and were off again across a hot, hot plain. The country was not Chinesy in the sense we think of it in Central China; rather it was more like home. A rolling land, green with fields of "galleon" which closely resembles our corn, occasional clumps of trees, some clay sand, and a few gullies and streams. The villages were of mud and stone with flat roofs, and the most distinctive feature of each was a shrine of stone, with a devil screen and a bell, overshadowed by stunted pines. Youngsters and a few lazy men collected in each village; half-clothed groups watched us curiously as we passed.

The trip across the plain was long and hot and tiresome, and by the time we had reached our first resting place, a temple fronted by what was once a nice lotus pond, we were so dripping outside and dry inside that we could scarcely eat tiffin. Eggs and sandwiches would not go down and warm beer assisted but little. A kettle of boiling water from the village, flavored with lime juice, relieved us somewhat, and two big watermelons bargained for by the head donkey-boy from the villagers, were the only really palatable things. The problem of water in China is a great one. All streams are apt to be polluted from the fields, and wells are not to be trusted. The people drink chiefly tea, which is the only safe thing to do. Even boiled water, however, can be dirty.

Rain in the Chili Foothills

The afternoon's tramp was relieved somewhat by a heavy shower, during which we took refuge under the huge gateway of an old tottering wall which once enclosed a village. The villagers welcomed us heartily, as they always do. One never lacks for a smile and a word of greeting from the half-naked coolies of China. Here also we had tea, made in a tinner's shop, and most welcome it was. Hot as we could bear it and sipped from chocolate-colored bowls.

And now we began to wade streams, or rather to step from stone to stone. We were in the foothills of the mountains. They had seemed blue in the distance; now we saw that they were green, jagged, rocky mountains liberally sprinkled with grass and shrubs. Sharp valleys wind up into them and up one of these we travelled. When we had crossed quite a large mountain stream a temple came in sight. It must have been once a most attractive place — picturesquely located at the foot of the mountains, interesting because of its idols and courtyards and priests; but nowadays it has become commercialized because so many parties such as ours are accustomed to stop there. There is even a barn like structure of two stories (without sides) which inhabits the former courtyard of the temple and which is most convenient for sleeping but very ugly. We preferred, however, to set up our cots on the terrace outside this structure — under the stars — the girls on one side of the entrance steps and the men on the other. Before supper we all had delightful baths; some in a hot spring which bubbles up in one of the outer rooms of the temple, some among the rocks where the mountain stream broadened and deepened into a beautiful pool.

The Jagged Hills

Supper that evening was not particularly successful. Uncle Alec, dressed in a long Chinese gown, mixed up a fine concoction of potatoes, onions, bacon and veal loaf but the little alcohol stove was not sufficient to cook the huge mess and after waiting and waiting until dark came and being further discouraged by an explosion of the alcohol bottle, we finally gave it up and ate sandwiches and eggs and coffee.

Nor indeed was our first night particularly successful. We saw a long black snake just before bedtime and that helped frighten the ladies on whose side he last crawled. And it was hot, and mosquitoes and flies and gnats were abundant. And all during the night the donkeys had fits of braying and a couple of dogs persistently tried to make away with our provisions.

In the morning it rained, and after our breakfast of the chow which had refused to cook the night before, we could not decide whether or not to start out. But finally it seemed to clear and we packed our wandering duds, put on our bathing suits and shoes and hats and were off again, our long cavalcade of walkers and riders and donkeys and donkey-boys wandering up through a rocky valley. We began to cross streams, stepping from stone to stone or riding the donkeys through the deeper parts but presently the streams became wider and deeper. Then they became more frequent. We gave up trying to keep our feet dry and trod nonchalantly across. Our shoes became sacks of soggy water. At one place a stream broadened out into a beautiful pool of clear green water at the foot of a towering precipice. Here we stopped long enough to swim.

Then came still more streams. We were really wandering up the beds of the streams, crossing again and again. It was cooler now and cloudier. Finally, a storm broke and we took refuge in the stone huts of a community of Chinese which fortunately were near. It was smelly inside and of course dirty, but it kept us dry. The old owner was hospitable as usual. He accepted a cigarette with shaky fingers, and accepted our money too on leaving, though insisting simultaneously that is was not necessary to give him anything. In the front courtyard of his home a little pomegranate tree was growing in an old Standard Oil tin. It is interesting to run across dwellers in the mountains. They always seem so cut off from the world, and yet withal so happy and content to live their lives away from other men. This old gentleman in blue cotton trousers (and nothing more) I am sure has heard nothing of the revolutions which have ravaged China in the past ten years; and how little the great political changes have affected his life!

It was still raining a bit when we started out again and so we pushed on and on without a stop for tiffin, always up and up and constantly rougher going. Finally, we crested the ridge and had a magnificent view back down the valleys and over the mountains to the plain in the distance. These jagged rocky mountains, covered with vegetation, remind one of parts of Japan and are by no means what one expects of great bare treeless China. To be sure there are but few trees on the mountains, but they are by no means bare, and certainly they are most distinctive and beautiful.

There are few experiences in life that equal mountain climbing. The long wearisome tramp, the steady climb, the endless plodding up-hill and clambering over rock, the last final effort and then the top when you look back on your toil and seem to be atop o' the world and to own it all, and you feel so healthy in the clear windswept air that you could shout with joy.

We did not stay on top our ridge long, but pushed on down an-other valley. Here we had another pleasure in store for us — the first mountain stream we had dared to drink, for in spite of our swims and the rain and much hot coffee and beer, we were still dry inside. Noth-ing can equal the thirst quenching quality of clear mountain water.

Not until four did we reach our destination this time another tem-ple, but much smaller and dirtier. We had been nine hours without food. Tiffin, tea and supper were combined and we had a splendid meal of baked beans, sausages, cocoa, bread and syrup. That night was cool and we made up for all the sleep we had missed.

The priest awakened us in the morning by insisting upon opening the temple door and having morning service. So after the donkey boy had removed such of our effects as blocked the way, the little long haired fellow, in a long-sleeved shirt proceeded to hold service by ring-ing the gong, shaking a bundle of lighted punk before the idol, and bowing to the floor. And we lay in our cots on the terrace just without and attended these Taoist Matins.

For the next two days we made this temple our headquarters, sleeping at night on the terrace of the temple proper, cooking in the temple yard with the brush and grass which all China uses for fuel, eating on the temple terrace, using the temple itself as a storehouse for our goods, and the temple side buildings and grounds as quarters for our donkeys and donkey boys. It made a fairly comfortable camping site though hot in the middle of the day, and rather noisy and smelly at night. But there was the consolation of a retreat in case of rain.

The temple was located at the foot of a conical rocky hill in a beautiful valley down which pushed a clear cold mountain stream. We drank the water of this stream without boiling it (most remarkable for China) and in the same stream washed our dishes, cleaned our teeth, shaved and bathed. And it made a better general wash bowl than civi-lization can furnish.

The Temple on Pei-nyiu-ting

On our first day at the temple a party climbed the highest mountain range nearby and spent all day in doing it but some of us stayed in camp and rested sore feet and swam in the mountain pools.

The next morning we climbed up the famous "Pei-nyui-ting." It is a mountain — a mountain of solid rock in the shape of an elongated dome and having at its very top a small Chinese temple which seems to be clinging to the sides of the precipitous rock. From the valley whence we started our climb, the great dome of rock looms up above the surrounding peaks as though it were inaccessible, but as you gradually approach nearer by clambering up the rocky bed of a tiny stream you see that there is a way up — but a way which has had to be prepared by the hand of man. For a time, it goes up the steep ravine

85

between two mountains — a path of rocks lined with bushes and vegetation and with a few clumps of beautiful pines. And then you reach a pass and can look far on the other side over range after range of hazy blue mountains, while overhead towers the almost perpendicular side of the Pei-nyiu-ting.

From the pass on up to the top the climb is over the very ridge of the mountain. At first it is merely from rock to rock and then overhead there looms a steep series of rocks which must be climbed by means of wooden ladders down the middle of which hang iron chains for "Safety First." When climbing them you feel like a fly on the face of the universe with the world spread out behind you, but the danger has been much over-exaggerated. A clear head and good hand grip are all that are necessary for absolute safety. Four of us in our party went up, including Mrs. Jordan, Stanard, myself and even one of our donkey-boys, whose energy and intrepidness in attempting the climb made us all wonder, for usually they are a lazy lot.

Priest on Top of Pei-nyiu-ting

At the end of the topmost ladder there is a gateway of stone with a little iron door which must be entered by climbing over a projecting ledge. It is really the only dangerous part of the climb, and at that is worse when you leave than when entering.

The rest of the way up is easy and you presently reach a temple built into the rock, presided over by an old priest who fits in perfectly with the quaintness and wildness of his mountain fastness.

The view from the top is splendid; you seem on top of the world, with green mountains spreading away in every direction and far off in the distance, the level greenness of the plain bordered by the white sand and the blue sea. There is some soil on top the rock and the priest has a little garden bordering his stone hut. And wonder of wonders — there is also a spring of water!

The way down the mountain after climbing over the ledge, is comparatively easy. We made good time and arrived for a late tiffin of bread and cheese and sardines and beer. Then the whole party packed up, and our procession of pack donkeys, walkers and riders made its way for two hours down the valley to a new camping spot. This time it was even more magnificent than before, for in addition to the beauty of the surrounding mountains, and the picturesqueness of a series of old Chinese watchtowers on the mountain tops, there was at this point a narrow defile filled with huge boulders through which the stream rushed in a series of little waterfalls and pools. The last pool was located almost under the huge overhanging rocks and its clear green water was fed by a beautiful fall. It was deep enough and large enough for swimming and has quite a reputation, being known as the "Dragon Pool," two Chinese characters being inscribed on the rocks to this effect.

In addition to all this the spot was made an ideal camping one by a fine grove of pine trees in which there was a clean little shrine which served as a storeroom for our food, a dressing place for the ladies, and even a retreat in case of rain, though to be sure we would have had to stand inside. But fortunately it rained only once and very briefly and we were able to spread our cots on the ground and to sleep out under the pine trees in perfect comfort.

This was our last night of the trip, for early next morning our party split and half of us started out for home. We each had a riding donkey and were able to make good time in spite of the rough going and long trip. The first two hours down the valley in which we had camped was one of the most magnificent trips I have ever made. The jagged surrounding mountains with their coating of green, the great rocks, the mountain stream with its falls and rapids and pools, and the early morning sun lighting it all up with long shadows and haziness, made a never-to-be-forgotten scene. It was very much like the mountains portrayed in Chinese paintings.

The valley gradually became wider and there were level spaces covered with green crops: galleon, maize, cotton, sesame. Near the very foot of the vale we ran across a Chinese village built of unhewn rocks, sprinkled with beautiful trees, and surrounded by growing crops. It was remarkably clean too and very picturesque. The villagers in their blue garments, with an occasional pair of red trousers which lent color, the little naked children, and the dogs and pigs, all ran out to greet us as we passed and stared us on our way.

We finally came out of the valley and began to cross the hot plain with its beautiful crops of green, which in their regularity and splendid state of cultivation could have taught a lesson to Kansas. We had tiffin in a fine grove of trees near another of the farming villages and then we settled down for the long hot ride of the afternoon. Little further happened, the only incident of note being when Mrs. Hoagland's big black donkey suddenly bucked and threw her backwards on her head. It jarred her up a bit but not seriously.

Late in the afternoon we crested a little hill and there spread out before us was the blue sea, the long slope sprinkled with verandared cottages, and the flags of Britain, France and America proclaiming that we were back in Peitaiho and civilization.

September 2, 1917, Peking
S. S. Tungchow

We are crossing the bar at the mouth of the river on which Tientsin is located and headed out to a yellow sea whose white caps and brisk breeze give promise of a little pitching. Ahead lies Shanghai and another year of work; behind lies a delightful Summer at the seashore. But more immediately in the past is a visit to Peking, pronounced by all tourists as the most interesting city in the East. This visit of mine, however, was not a sightseeing one; last Winter I "did" Peking in that way. This time I was fortunate in seeing more of the social side and my impressions are of Peking as the Legation City.

In Peitaiho I met several young Americans who are Student Interpreters in the Legation and they asked me to stop in Peking for a day or so while on the way back to Shanghai. I was particularly glad to do so because of the recent Revolution in the city.

So we went up to Peking from Peitaiho by the night train, travelling much as we might have done at home. I was there for two days, living in the Student's Mess of the Legation, meeting old friends and making new, wandering about the city, doing some curio shopping, playing tennis at the Peking Club, going to the cinema, etc. Once we went out to see what was left of Chang Hsun's house, after it had been bombarded during the fighting last July.* There was not much. The interior had been completely demolished and only the outside Compound wall still stood complete. The remarkable thing was that there was very little evidence of the shelling in the immediate neighborhood. A few trees showed naked limbs and there were bullet marks on walls, but the great Imperial City wall, crowned with its yellow tiles, stood apparently untouched a hundred yards away. Evidently the Righteous Army of the Republic had done excellent shooting.

Across the Jade Fountain Canal, however (a smelly ditch in fact) there was more tangible evidence that there had been fighting. A large Chinese junk filled to the brim with fighting men and gigantic figures of hideous old style warriors was surrounded by a curious crowd of Chinese. The whole creation was of paper and designed to be burned in memory of those who were killed in the revolution.

Paper Boat

*see End Notes

89

The life in Peking must be a delightful one in many ways. All diplomatic centers are gay and Peking has the reputation of being especially so. Of course since the war there has been but little entertaining, but even in wartime and in Summer, I could perceive an air of gaiety about the place which is distinctly different from any other foreign center in China. Then too it is even more International than Shanghai and the representatives of the various countries are more truly representative. The Peking Club was most interesting because of this. Italians, French, British and Americans were on the courts, and each playing their own style of tennis.

The American Legation impressed me as something of the center of the life in Peking. The American Minister, with the resignation of the French Ambassador, has become Dean of the Diplomatic Corps, and America is held in high regard by the Chinese. In the recent troubles Mr. Reinsch played a large part in the diplomacy which goes with all such events in China. As I was staying in part of the Legation I saw something of what it is like from the inside and heard more.

I left Peking with regret and really had something of a homesick spell for the north and all the friends I have made there. As the train sped across the great plain to Tientsin, it was quite like leaving part of America to travel to another part, though I cannot quite reconcile Shanghai as yet as a home.

In Tientsin that night however, I might well have imagined myself in an American city. After taking my luggage from the train to the boat by rickshaw and eating a cold supper on board ship, I took rickshaw again in search of stamps for postals and for some excitement for the evening. And on the street I met a Peitaiho friend who told me of a prize fight that was coming off that night between Art Martell of Australia and one of the American soldiers in Tientsin. So we went up to a large "go-down" which had been converted into an arena and which was already crowded with men varying in type from American soldiers in uniform to Britishers in dinner jackets. And we saw a splendid fight, in which the soldier won out and was carried off on the shoulders of his compatriots amid cheers which shook the roof. Not quite like China!

September 1917
St. John's University
(see End Notes)

Iarrived back from my Summer vacation in north China to
find that I was the last of the faculty to return. As I rolled
in my rickshaw through the Compound entrance gate, and
up the driveway to the main group of buildings, it was late
afternoon and I could see nearly the whole of the foreign community
on the tennis courts. Our courts are of turf, beautifully situated in the
center of the great group of grey and red brick buildings which constitute the University, and commanding views also of the trees and lawn
for which our Compound is notable in Shanghai. The tennis players
in their cool whites, against the green of the grass and trees, a green
which looked particularly vivid to me after a Summer in the yellow
north, gave a most pleasing effect, resembling a country club rather
than the missionary institution as generally pictured. Those afternoon
hours on the courts mean much to us all; after seven hours of mental
labor one needs just the relaxation and physical exercise which they
give.

Shanghai was in the midst of a hot spell during the few days pre-
ceding the opening of college. Shanghai hot spells can scarcely be surpassed on the globe. The heaviness of the atmosphere is sickening;
the heat is terrific. Even with the impetus of a healthful Summer, the
heat seems to grasp you and pull you down to a state of inaction and
depression. At least it affects me in that way; some people are so con-
stituted they thrive in it.

On the Chinese themselves the heat seems to have little effect. You
see coolies with bared heads in a sun which would knock a white man
down in half an hour; the students can continue their work through
the worst of it seemingly unaffected.

During these hot days there was plenty of work to be done. Entrance examinations must be held to the College and Middle School; Conditional Examinations must be given to those who had failed in courses last year; new students must be classified. And so while the sun poured out its molten heat, and the white gowned students slowly gathered, we of the faculty labored and sweated, made out papers, presided over reeking classrooms while the students put down their knowledge on paper, corrected those papers and turned in the marks to an office which was approaching in activity the pit of a Stock Exchange.

By now the Compound was alive with students. They came on foot, in rickshaws, in autos. Their effects came on wheelbarrows, the ill-kempt coolies panting under their huge loads of pig skin boxes, of baskets and bags of clothes, of desks and bedding. Often the owner sat on the side of the barrow in true old fashioned style, balancing his great load of goods on the other.

By six o'clock of the opening day the stream of incoming students had reached its climax and by the time the tower bell had rung its last call for assembly at six-thirty, the last student quickened his rickshaw coolie up the driveway with hurried "auh-sauhs," and hurried in for roll-call. The year had opened.

September 9, 1917 First Classes

First classes on the opening of college are not taken very seriously in a studious way. But in other respects I am inclined to think they mean a great deal. It is the time above all others when the students "size-up" the teachers, and the teacher cannot but be conscious of this. This is as true in a Chinese classroom as at home.

Chatter ceases as you approach the door, and with true courtesy the class rises as a body to greet you and sits down as you take your seat in your desk chair. They are a serious looking company: respectful, deadly in earnest, and most quiet and orderly. They wear long blue cotton gowns, their trousers of white are gathered in at the ankle, their shoes are of black cloth and pointed. The hair is straight and black, short-cropped save for someone who is a "sport" and has let his grow long and slicked it down with grease. The faces vary in contour but have a tendency to roundness, cheek bones high under the eyes, noses flat and with no bridge, the eyes tending to almond shape. It is not a pleasing face from an Anglo-Saxon viewpoint, yet here and there are ones distinctly handsome, and the clear olive complexion of the younger boys, particularly in combination with the brightness of their black eyes, is most attractive. There is an oriental calm in all the faces which you feel you would like to break through. As they survey you with that stoical expression, you wonder what is going on back in their heads. You will be a fortunate man if you ever know. In two years I have never broken through. The best that one can do is to reach a state of complete indifference to their seeming indifference.

To the teacher new to China the roll-call of the class is an obstacle hard to be surmounted. The Chinese characters denoting the names of the students have been put into an English spelling which is called Romanization. These strange looking words, such as Waung Ooong-Kyuin or Khoong Kyuin-tsien or Ng Ths-ngauh, are by no means pronounced as they look (which in itself would be hard enough); there is a set of rules for their interpretation, and it takes study to learn it.

So the new teacher is confronted by a class whose names are as incomprehensible as their faces are imperturbable. Ingenious new teachers have been known to number each scholar, and likewise number the class book and the classroom seats. It's an easy way out of the difficulty, but just as hard to get out of as was the original problem. After a year in China one teacher is still numbering.

And so first classes are held. And the roll is called and books discussed and work assigned. And the class sizes up the teacher, and the teacher the class — and neither knows what the other thinks. And the teacher rises, the class rising also as a parting courtesy, and he walks out briskly and goes to another class. The work of the year has begun.

November 17, 1917
Funeral of a Rich Man

葬礼

Preparations have been made in Shanghai for what promises to be the greatest funeral ceremony that has ever been held in the memory of the foreigner in China. The cause of all the display was once a leading light in the Revolution of six years ago which made China a so-called Republic, a man who by a terrific governmental "squeeze" and by judicial investments in the railroads and steamboat lines when they were in their very infancy, made a fortune which would be considered large even in America. But in the midst of enjoying his tremendous wealth he died.

That was a year ago. Since then he has reposed in a huge coffin covered with beautiful red embroidery at his residence on Bubbling Well Road. And now his wife and daughters and sons and probably too his sisters and his cousins and his aunts, have decided to make at least one move towards burying him. They have decided to transfer his body to Soochow. But when he was alive the great man moved in state, and so now his last journey is to be made a truly memorable one.

To this end the family has expended huge sums of money; the exact amount varying with the credulity of the last rumor-spreader, but at all events well up in the hundred thousands. What it has been spent on — in addition to some $50,000 to be given the Municipal Council for the privilege of using the streets of the International Settlement for a few hours — perhaps I can best explain by trying to describe a visit I paid this afternoon to the home of the deceased. I should explain that his home has been thrown open for inspection (the relatives being very proud of the stupendous preparations) and that is how we were able to go in, the presentation of a personal card being sufficient ticket of admission, as is the case so often in China.

At the entrance gate, a huge tower constructed of white cloth in closely gathered festoons and of much lacquer, blazoned forth that this was the house of mourning. A great crowd had collected in front and their faces were lighted up by a glare of hundreds of electric lights and gave a fitting initial atmosphere to the pagan spectacle.

The entrance drive within the gates had been converted by the liberal use of cotton cloth and of white festoons upon a bamboo framework, into a long enclosed passageway, blazing with lights and stretching away in the distance. Moreover, as we advanced down this corridor of mourning (for white is to the Chinese the funereal color) we came upon other passageways of a similar nature at right angles; the whole front compound having been turned into labyrinth of white corridors.

Lining the walls of these seemingly endless passageways were the various banners and instruments to be carried in the procession on the morrow. Here were a series of long satin banners with characters; here were strange flags and emblems of white; long racks held glittering arrays of old fashioned spears with heads like those of Roman Legions; other racks were full of huge umbrellas with embroidered curtains dropping from their edges like the canopies of Cleopatra. Here were hundreds of figures made of paper, clever imitations of fighting men, of men on horseback, of automobiles; there were similar figures constructed of flowers, or of greens, the capping one being a huge locomotive constructed of chrysanthemums!

At one place, there was a recess in the passage and in it rested the tremendous catafalque which was to carry the coffin. It was a magnificent creation in red, with beautifully embroidered dragons in gold, and resting upon great red-lacquered poles which spread out and out like the roots of an oak, until there was room for sixty men to bear the weight upon their shoulders. In another recess were the funeral offerings of friends, consisting of various structures and figures of paper and of flowers, the most pretentious being an heroic statue of the deceased, very well produced of bronze-colored wood.

All these passageways were jammed with people, a pushing, sightseeing crowd which savored gaiety rather than sorrow. There were visiting Chinese by the score (it is said that Shanghai is filled with visitors for the funeral), a fair scattering of foreigners, a motley crew of coolies making final preparations, the servants of the house clad in funeral white, other coolies rushing through the crowd with great savory dishes of fish and bowls of rice (we happened to arrive at chow time), and last but by no means least, the retainers and bandmen who had been hired for the procession. These were clad in various uniforms, varying from a natty modification of a modern Belgian soldier, to the ancient gown and hat of the Manchu Dynasty. Most of them were this latter type — indeed the whole arrangements for the funeral were decidedly old fashioned Chinese. Everything was most pagan and extreme, just as it might have been before the foreigner came with his strange modern ideas and religion.

Within the house itself the same magnificence and gaudiness was maintained, reaching its climax in the shrine of the dead man, a table magnificently decorated and covered with candles, burning incense, ancestral tablets and so forth, and backed by an embroidered picture of the deceased. Before this shrine the visiting friends (not the onlookers such as we were) did their obeisance to his memory by three deep "head-knocking" bows, and behind it rested the red covered coffin of the great man, cut off by curtains from the curious (who could, however, peek in!), and surrounded by his mourning family in their white robes of sorrow. (When I peeked, however, they seemed a very cheerful bunch).

The effect of the whole was one of wasteful "display"; of huge expenditure for embroidered baubles and paper gods; heathenism carried to the extreme. And there was a further atmosphere about it all which is harder to define and yet more definitely felt — I mean a certain flavor of medievalism. The spears and lances; the ancient banners; the aimless crowd jostled by servants bearing platters of steaming meat; a glimpse we had of the kitchen with Chinese stoves and shouting menials, its fire-lit steam amidst the dull light of sputtering candles; the scores of retainers sitting about in uniform or eating at rough board tables; all this combined to give the atmosphere of the Middle Ages as we picture them in our imagination.

November 26, 1917
Explosions in the Night

爆竹

It is very, very seldom that the Orient of Reality approximates that gorgeous, mysterious, terrifying Orient of our Western Imagination. Indeed, the newcomer to the East is apt to think of his previous conception as founded on an entirely erroneous view. Later, however, he has experiences which more nearly resemble his dream pictures. Such occasions are apt to be in rainy weather, for at that time there is decidedly more "atmosphere" — more dreamers and mystery. But they may come at any time and most unexpectedly.

In the middle of last night, I found myself suddenly awake and filled with that dread of the unknown which only comes on such occasions or when we are children. I felt an uncontrollable fear of the thing that had awakened me, without knowing what that thing was. Then as my senses gradually became more alive I could hear weird wailing strains of strange music. Instinctively and without being far enough awake to think of being in China, I recognized the wailing flutes and the beating tom-toms as Oriental, and instantly all my "home" conception of the Orient was before me.

A moment later the spell was broken by the sound of an explosion, closely followed by a second and louder one. I immediately recognized the typical Chinese firecracker and was brought back to complete consciousness. My picture of the Orient vanished, the indescribable dread went with it, and I turned over in bed in disgust at being thus deceived. But I could not sleep, for the abominable firecrackers continued at intervals and the weird, sad music was played in between bursts of the louder noise.

This morning I learned that nearly the whole Compound was awakened by the same performance. It was taking place in our nearby delightful little village of Zou Ka Doo in honor of someone who had died in the past four or five years. It seems that he died at the inconsiderate time of 4 A.M., hence all such festivals in his honor must be held at that hour. We have one little group of houses which project directly in front of one of our dormitories and they are in the habit of giving us many early morning concerts of this same general variety.

Zou Ka Doo from Mann Hall

Shops at Zou Ka Doo

Meat Shop

Kitchen

Tea Shop

Rattan Shop

November 19, 1917
Dr. Ling I-Sung

Whenever I feel the need of a reconsecration to my work here, all that is necessary is a simple visit to Ling I-Sung's (Dr. Lincoln's) Dispensary. While we are trying in the school and college classroom to meet the mental needs of Chinese students, and to instill in them a new spiritual growth by methods which I fear at times are rather academic, he is getting at the very heart of China's greatest and most immediate need by alleviating their suffering. Our work is in theory and too often but touches the outer surface of things; his is intensely practical and reaches human nature in one of its most receptive moods.

Every day there comes to his little suite of working rooms a file of suffering coolies from our filthy neighboring village of Zou Ka-Doo. They are afflicted with innumerable forms of those loathsome skin diseases so prevalent where soap and water and sanitation are unknown. They are of all ages and of both sexes, but without exception they are of extreme ignorance and filthy in body. But they are human — very, very human, and that is what we notice in them as the doctor deftly cleans their horrible sores and binds them up. One old coolie has labored all his life in his garden patch. Now he has great ulcers on the shins of both legs, probably brought on originally (the doctor says) by syphilis and augmented by neglect and dirt. They are terribly painful, but the old man only screws his mouth the tighter and makes deeper the wrinkles about his eyes. When we ask him his name he answers with a smile and adds some information about his business.

The next in line is a mother holding a wailing infant. Her face too betrays her ignorance, but as the doctor probes a deep hole in the baby's face and he kicks and squirms and screams, she holds him close to her breast and croones him in that mother talk which is the same the world over.

And so it goes. All morning long the doctor and his assistant tend that waiting line of suffering humanity. This was a fine, bright day and he treated ninety cases, helped bring more light into ninety homes. That thought is what helps me; makes me determine to put new effort and life into my work that it may be of more real and practical service.

November 29, 1917
Thanksgiving Day

感恩节

We have just returned by the evening train from a Thanksgiving Holiday spent in Soochow. This makes my second visit to Soochow this Fall and my fifth since I came to China, but it is a Chinese city of which one never wearies. Aside from the relief of getting "up-country" and away from the gaudy, semi-foreign brazenness of Shanghai, there is a fascination in the city itself. It has been called the "Venice of the East" because of its many canals and its picturesqueness, and the Chinese themselves say of it: "Heaven is above, Soochow beneath."

To the newcomer to China it is a typical city. One detrains outside the smoldering old city wall and is held immediately by the picturesqueness of the moat without the walls, filled with it traffic of boats and junks; by the winding wall with its bastions and battlements, vine covered and crumbling with age; and by the tops of several fine pagodas which dot the huge space within. Once within the ponderous city gates, after being conveyed down the stone paved road by rickshaw or open carriage (for ten coppers or forty respectively!), there succeeds the usual narrow twisting streets of a Chinese city, with the open shops, the crowded hanging signs, the pushing shouting pedestrians and still noisier vendors and burden carriers, donkeys and sedan chairs, and with the children and beggars, dogs and smells and a thousand other little things which make a Chinese thoroughfare the most human sight in the world. But these streets are more interesting than those in other cities, for constantly they are crossing the dirty, traffic laden canals. They cross them on humpbacked stone bridges which architecturally are beautiful but for practical purposes are most inconvenient, being useable only by sedan chairs, donkeys, and pedestrians.

I wish I could put on paper the impressions of a Chinese city but I have never seen it thoroughly portrayed. Reduced to simplest terms there is a sense of crowding which surpasses that of any cities in the west, houses jammed together, streets almost impassable, people everywhere; a feeling that you are constantly confined in a small space and unable to get out of it. There is no possibility of viewing the city as a whole and no matter where you go, you are bound in by the narrow streets and the overhanging houses; an impression of the fecundity of Oriental life and at the same time of its wretchedness. There are more people to the square yard than in New York and nearly all are poorly dressed and show in their faces and bearing, poverty, hard work and lack of hygiene; the feeling that the people are willing and eager to become your friends — for in spite of an occasional "Yang Quei-Ts" (foreign devil) muttered as you pass, and the very evident fear of the children, there are always smiles when you smile and a ready response if you address them in their own language; and finally a confusion of some of the senses brought about the unaccustomed sights, the constant babel of strange sounds, the many smells so obnoxious to the Western nose, and the breaking of our American ideas of propriety.

It is always a great relief after being in a Chinese street for some time to break into the quiet, incense-scented openness of a great Temple court. Here one encounters the beauty of Chinese roofs; the hideous great plaster gods; the dusty dilapidated state of everything; the contentment (and dirtiness sometimes) of the quiet shaven headed priests; the heathenism of the gods, the chants, and the gongs. And it is a still greater relief to climb up on the city wall (it is usually of banked earth within) and to look down on the black tiled roofs of the crowded city and breathe once more the untainted air of the open country. But even the sense of the peace and seeming purity of a city wall may be rudely shattered if one finds, as we did this afternoon, an old rice sack containing the dead body of a new-born infant, perhaps left there because he was an unwelcome guest to a poverty-stricken home.

December 15, 1917
Shanghai Winter

When a really cold day comes, then do we fully realize that Shanghai is in the Tropics; for our vegetation, our houses and we ourselves are not made for real Winter. The palm trees seem to shrink and shrivel; the camphor tree is far too green and out of season; our rooms develop unknown cracks, our miserable little stoves seem but makeshifts; and our bodies shrink and our chests contract against all the efforts of our will.

But the Chinese seem as stoical as ever. They put on another layer of clothing, grow so much nearer the general shape of a football, lengthen their sleeves until their hands entirely disappear. The weather is seldom a topic of conversation to Chinese when they first meet; I suppose through the centuries they have developed a racial trait of such indifference to the variations of their miserable climate that it is no longer interesting to them. Instead, they ask a stranger his age and home conditions, and make interesting conversation about food and money.

But with the "foreigner," the "outside country man," it is quite different. On cold damp nights he finds it impossible to keep warm. Bed clothes by the pound; bed socks, heavy pajamas and bathrobes, do not keep out the cold. Many are the methods guaranteed by the inventor to keep out that frigid stream which flows down like mountain water between the head, the bedclothes and the pillow. But none really works.

And in the daytime it is even worse. Next to the stove is the only comfortable spot. Most of our classrooms have little iron stoves with pipes out of the window, but they roar away impotently against the cold which seeps in every window and door. So we pull on our gloves, snuggle down into our overcoats, and try to be as philosophic as our students.

December 28, 1917
A Lunar Eclipse

St. John's is located about five miles from the center of the International Settlement, off to itself among the huge Chinese country population of this flat Yangtze River delta. The road to it is euphoniously named the "Bubbling Well Road" and is famous in China as the location of the homes of the wealthy among the foreigners in Shanghai ("foreigner" meaning "other than Chinese"). For three miles it might be thought a street in the suburbs of an English city and it is possible to ride thus far in a so-called "tram." But at the Bubbling Well itself, which is a Chinese Temple with a dirty well in front, the street ends, and there succeeds Jessfield Road, which winds out into the Chinese countryside, gradually shaking itself free of the homes of the foreigners and finally passing through the center of the Chinese village I have previously mentioned in these pages, until it brings one to the beautiful Compound of St. John's University.

This Jessfield Road is two miles long, and so we are accustomed to make use of that overgrown baby-carriage known as the "rickshaw," pulled by some poor, ragged coolie. They trot the distance willingly for twelve coppers. But on cold nights when we have plenty of time to spare, we sometimes walk out to St. John's from the tram terminus, waving aside the rickshaws which flock around one like awkward turkeys demanding food.

Tonight was such a night. We are in the midst of our five day Christmas holiday and I had been in town visiting friends and was returning to college. The sun had set, but it was bitterly cold, so I decided to walk the two miles for the exercise and the warmth. As soon as I had passed the foreign houses, and the road was free of trees, I happened to glance back at the moon and saw that it was in almost total eclipse, with a great curved shadow covering practically all of its brilliant face. And almost immediately I became conscious that strange things were happening through the whole Chinese countryside. From every little village and every mud-tiled hut scattered over that flat, ugly expanse of muddy fields and great conical grave mounds, there arose exploding firecrackers. The whole country seemed to be on a 4th of July rampage — widespread and unceasing. The strange effect of this general fusillade was heightened by long drawn-out wails which arose from several quarters and by the sound of a gong beating wildly in a distant temple.

It was evident that the country people were alarmed by the eclipse of the moon and were doing their best to restore it to its normal condition. As I walked on, the signs of excitement were even more evident. Women and children stood about the road and talked loudly; pedestrians and wheelbarrow riders gesticulated violently. And when the village loomed up, things were at their height. The whole population of the dark, grimy town was on the single street. I had to dodge through a mass of ragged, thickly padded Chinese. They were all excited, though not particularly terrified.

In front of one poor, one-room home the family "Lares and Penates," consisting of a tray of pewter vessels and two red candles, had been brought into the street. The candles were lighted, and the family and numerous friends were bowing before them. One man was kow-towing all the way to the ground.

In the central part of the village street, where the people and lights and smells were thickest, they were sending off the town's contribution of firecrackers. Chinese crackers are different from their namesakes in America. Each cracker has two bangs; one which sends it up into the air trailing sparks, and a second and louder explosion at the highest point of ascent. The whole village street and the very heavens above were full of crackers, the number "one" bang, followed by resounding flashes and thundering of the number "two" bangs, and the air was thick with smoke, sparks, and unburnt cracker cases. Through this barrage I had to walk, and somehow I managed to reach our Compound without losing my coat-tails or my foreign dignity. Then gradually the moon unfolded from the earth's shadow and the noise of China ceased. The natives had succeeded in driving away the dog which was devouring their beloved moon.

People of the Chinese Countryside

Girl in Doorway near Soochow

Blind Beggar, Hangchow

Chestnut Vendor, Canton

Wrinkled Man, Location Unknown

Sedan Chair Coolie, Yangchow

Baby in a Stand Barrel, Location Unknown

Man in Doorway, Location Unknown

February, 1918
A Hunting Trip on the Grand Canal

大运河

Our hunting party, planned with the intent of enjoying the Chinese New Year vacation by decreasing the number of ducks, pheasant and geese along the Grand Canal, collected gradually as the express north from Shanghai sped on its way one damp Winter morning. The Story Teller was the first on board. He was well primed for the trip and started in on the Long One and myself as we boarded the train with our motley luggage of warm clothes and bedding, guns, shells. The Yankee and Newly-Wed joined us at Soochow, overshadowed, however, by the Southerner, whose magnificent dog (inappropriately named June) immediately classed him as a real hunter.

The six of us made ourselves happy with books and cards, and a tiffin of Chinese rice and egg, until we reached Chinkiang on the Yangtze. So far had been comparative luxury in travel, a foreign-managed railway through Chinese country and with most of the foreign conveniences, but here, at this little Chinese port, our troubles began.

To begin with our luggage did not come on our train. Rule number one when travelling in China, viz: "See your luggage on the train with your own eyes," had been neglected. Result: the baggage officials had seen fit to leave the most valuable suit-cases and bedding behind. We telegraphed and they promised to send it on the next train.

But the delay brought more trouble. We were due to take a launch leaving at three, which would cross the Yangtze and tow us up the Grand Canal to Yangchow, the starting point of our real trip. The Prime Mover and the Old Hand were waiting for us there with our houseboat, also with a hot supper and warm beds. But the next train was not due in time to catch the launch.

The Yankee and the Southerner, both experts in the dialect we had now run into (almost a complete change of tongue in a six-hour railway journey) went to use strategy on the launch officials. They prevailed on them to hold the launch until 3:30.

Naturally enough the train was just sufficiently late to miss the launch even then. But we were happy for we now had all our luggage. Six coolies staggered under the weight of trunks and suitcases, guns and typewriters and shells, great bundles of chow and bedding and folding cots.

We chartered a small Chinese junk with special coolie pullers and promises of much "cumshaw" if they reached Yangchow before twelve. It was a typical Chinese river boat: square at the ends, heavy timbered, mast at a rakish angle, a great square sail, a small cabin amidships, full of cracks, filthy and black and smooth with the wear of years. When we had walked on planks two hundred yards over the mud where the Yangtze had receded during the dry Winter months, and boarded it with all our possessions, there was not much room left for exercise.

As the Winter twilight quickly deepened, we crept through the crowded junks which lined the flat river banks and out into the mighty yellow flood of the Yangtze. Night had fallen by the time we had sculled and sailed across the half mile of muddy water and nosed into the quite narrow entrance of the canal. One could not have desired a more picturesque introduction to the Grand Canal. Junks with great square sails creaked by through the misty night, others crept down the canal and put out on the great river, there was a subdued hum of voices in the boats tied up at the bank, an occasional strident shout rent the stillness as boats in motion threatened collision.

Grand Canal

Our trackers now went ashore with their lines and started the difficult task of pulling us up against the current. We could see their paper lantern far ahead as we sat in the little cabin eating our supper of crackers and cheese. It was fairly comfortable within. The six of us, the "boy" and the dog, crowded the dirty little cockpit, but that helped keep us warm. Also we had an oil stove going, which gave further heat and light. We passed several hours telling stories, singing songs and twanging on mandolins.

But that grew tiresome eventually, even the Story Teller and Newly-Wed began to run short of tales, and so at one of the Custom stations, where a drum was beating lustily, four of our party went ashore to walk, leaving Yankee and myself to guard the boat. We promptly rolled up in blankets, ran the risk of the dirt and bugs and lay down on the hard bunks to sleep.

117

I awoke with that bewildered sensation which sometime accompanies the half-awake time in strange surroundings. And surely the surroundings were unusual enough to cause the feeling. The little 6 by 8 by 10 cabin with its smooth-worn boards, plastered in places with gaudy paintings of gods, the oil stove sputtering and smelling bad as it flickered out, a dog snoring in the corner, the steady *puf*, the boatmen overhead, the creak of the rudder in the rear were enough to bewilder one's sound senses, and in my half-awake state it took me many minutes to find myself.

It was 2 A.M. before we reached the tumble down huts which marked the outskirts of Yangchow and tied up at the muddy bank. Then our boatmen refused to go inside the city on the side canal. We knew that the city gate would refuse us admittance and we were in a quandary. We dared not leave all the luggage; our four fellow travelers were nowhere to be seen in the dark, narrow streets bordering the canal; and there was no way for us to carry goods. We did the only possible thing: pulled out our own bedding, unrolled in on the hard bunks of the cabin, and lay down to pass the rest of the night.

Early the same morning we were up again, the boatmen obtained some coolies for us, and they loaded our effects on their three wheelbarrows. Then we bumped along the rough, slippery streets of the city, through a misty rain, past the open shops and houses where old women were cooking the morning rice, through the city gate, the soldiers smiling at us as a welcome, and finally reached the Mission Compound of the Chung Wha Sheng Kung Wei. The cleanliness and quiet and peace of that Compound and its semi-foreign houses was like a haven of rest after all the dirt and noise we had been experiencing. A hot breakfast and the warm welcome of our host and friends was also good.

That same morning, we started our real trip. Our home for the next ten days we found to be a large river boat, a heavy timbered affair with two masts. There was a long cabin amidships, split up into three small rooms. One was rigged up as a living and dining room, with a small iron stove and a Chinese table; another was just large enough for two double bunks; the third served as a kitchen. The crew of six and our two "boys" and cook were to sleep somewhere in the rear of all this.

Prime Mover was responsible for the hiring and fitting out of the venerable ship and he was lucky to find anything as good at New Year time. Together with Old Hand he had been bagging supplies for the past two days. The addition of these two now gave us eight men in our party, about nine servants and crew, two dogs, and two chickens which we discovered were to be slaughtered as a sacrifice on New Year's Eve.

We "opened boat" as the Chinese say, about noon, and our pullers slipped along the tow path in a cold rain as they tried to tow us against the swift current. After tiffin we had made enough headway to be in the open country, so we put on our hunting clothes and heavy boots and leggings and landed to look for game.

Our Boat

The rain had turned into a wet snow which beat into our faces as we went forward in a wide skirmish line across the country. The whole scene was a symphony in brown: hillocks of sere grass, ploughed fields of dark brown loam intersected with the paths of mud, conical grave mounds covered with withered shrubbery, leafless trees in little clumps, groups of brown thatched cottages. The people and the dogs furnished the only relief; the former were clad in the blue cotton universal in China and the latter, which barked at us fiercely at every house, were gray or black.

I soon found myself in hard luck, for when we fetched up a pheasant my gun missed fire. A second time it did the same thing. It was a borrowed gun and apparently no good, so I consulted with Prime Mover and together we started back to the boat to send a messenger back to Yangchow for another gun.

Shooting Pheasant

As we walked along the muddy towpath, up and down the slippery hills bordering the canal, I saw one of the Chinese dogs worrying at a bundle. At our approach he dragged it off inland. I was curious to see what the bundle of straw contained and walked over to drive the dog off. He snarled off and waited at a distance. It was a dead baby! A poor little year old infant partly exposed in his bundle of burial straw, the throat and all the lower jaw eaten away by the ravenous work. I wanted

120

to shoot the beast as he waited to get at his prey again, but we feared it might cause trouble with the neighboring people who probably owned him, so all we could do was to pile up a funeral cairn of stones and clods of earth over the mutilated body of the child.

February 10, 1918

By the next morning it had cleared off cold. We slept through the last blissful hours of a splendid night's rest to the steady tramp of straw-sandalled feet overhead where the poling coolies walked back and forth. Then a pretense at washing, slipping on the outer garments we had laid aside, a hearty breakfast and we were ready for the day's hunting.

At the point where we went ashore the canal widened out until it was almost a lake, a beautiful stretch of almost clear water with the white junk sails flashing in the sunlight, and a temple with its red poles lending the proper Chinese touch to the shore. There was also a hilly island which had as a spine, a long clump of feathery bamboo, still green.

Norton Inquiring the Way

We saw pheasants against the skyline on one of the hills even before a small boat had landed us. So, in skirmish line, we began a careful combing of the islet. The Long One and I broke through a clump of bamboo and stumbled upon a little gray brick hut, thatch-roofed and fitting in perfectly with its surroundings. An old woman was hanging blue clothes on the bushes, there were chickens about the door, the front yard commanded a view of the great stretch of the canal; the only thing which broke the peacefulness of the scene was the usual Chinese cur, which snarled at my heels as I snapped a picture of the Long One talking with the old woman.

Meanwhile the others had scared up pheasant and we had some fine shots as they went by. Luck was not with us. The Long One missed a bird which came straight at him as he hid behind a grave hillock, and I seemed to be a hoodoo for guns; the pump gun I had borrowed from the Southerner missed fire four times in the next half hour. So I began to use my camera instead. Almost instantly the sun went in.

We crossed over a branch canal on a small boat for three coppers and climbed the embankment. A remarkable scene lay spread out below us on the other side. The country for miles inland was below the level of the canal and consequently was in itself split up by canals. The land itself was literally peppered with conical grave mounds covered with withered grass and interspersed with little clumps of funeral trees. Most of the mounds were scattered about indiscriminately, but some few were arranged in family lots, bounded by a horseshoe-shaped mound.

In this strange countryside we fetched up many pheasant. They are hard birds to hit, getting up almost under your feet with a great whir-r-r-r and speeding away in a rising flight like an aeroplane. They usually light again within some hundred yards but it almost impossible to find them, for they can run more swiftly than a man and are experts at dodging behind grave mounds. The color of the hens also is a camouflage against the brown grass. Sometimes you will be looking at a spot and suddenly a bird will rise out of what was seemingly but vegetation. The cocks are more easily distinguished for they are brilliantly colored. Indeed, they are a remarkably beautiful bird, with wonderful shades of red, blue, violet and gray, and with a long streaming tail of gray and white. In size they are about the same as a tame chicken, in fact they are so similar that the Chinese call pheasant "Ya-kyi," which means "wild chicken."

The country presently became more normal, with the tiny fields of plowed land, little mud tiled villages and the everlasting canals. Through this we hunted until noon when a large temple on the canal embankment marked the beginning of a city. The canal had entirely changed its character. I laughed at my former conception of the Grand Canal as a long straight stretch of narrow water through the flat country. Here the canal was narrow but it had a beautiful curve and its yellow stream was running like a millrace. The banks on each side were very high, some thirty feet perhaps. One bank was bounded with stone and along it stretched a Chinese town; the other was grass covered and planted with a row of old willows. Beyond this dyke, water stretched away into a wide lake, dotted with islands. The canal was crowded with shipping, some few boats being pulled up stream very, very slowly by coolies who bent to their task at a 45-degree angle; but the great majority were going down with the current. Their great square sails were set and they flew swiftly around the curve of the canal, like a never ceasing flock of huge white winged birds.

Village Along the Grand Canal

We found our boat among the hundreds tied along the canal bank. It was recognizable by the American flag flying from the mast head and the flag never looks better than in a foreign country. Chinese call it the "Flowery Flag" and America is the "Kingdom of the Flowery Flag."

After a splendid tiffin we started out again after pheasants, going through the narrow town, down the dyke and scattering off in the

123

countryside of ploughed fields, grave mounds and villages. We started
up several pheasant and in chasing them, the Long One and myself
went pretty far inland and became separated from the rest of the party.

Then began a series of adventures with that bane of cross-country
travelers in China — the canals. Looked at in retrospect they are humorous, but at the time they were exasperating and bid fair to be disas-
trous. Our troubles started when we found ourselves boxed in the "T"
of two wide canals in the open country. We were contemplating risking
a jump across a place where there had once been a bridge, rather than
walk back several miles, when an old countryman came out. He tried
to tell us all about the lay of the land and we in turn fired away wildly
in our Shanghai dialect explaining our difficulties. Neither got much
satisfaction out of speech, but our gestures were much more successful. Finally, he understood that we wanted a boat, and he impressed
upon us that he had one and that we must go far in order to get out of
the network of canals. The long drawn "A-aa-h-h" and the deep bow
which he made when this dialogue got across would have made a hit
on the vaudeville stage.

At last his boat came, a narrow clean little vessel propelled by a
boy and an old woman. They took us down the canal and demurred
when we wanted to land on the other side of the "T." But we insisted,
paid them, and landed, for it was cold and we preferred walking. Ten
minutes later we were kicking ourselves for not keeping that boat, for
we found ourselves on the inside of a figure "G." Everywhere we went
there was a canal at right-angles until we almost gave up in despair.
Then we managed to get across one small canal and began to hasten
inland to get around the series and reach the Grand Canal embankment. Another canal blocked us! But fortunately there was a house and
a boat. They ferried us across.

It was rapidly getting dark now and our difficulties were multiply-
ing. Our Shanghai Chinese failed again and again to bring satisfactory
results in asking directions. Nor could we understand the natives. One
thing we could get across was the name of the village on the Grand
Canal where our boat was to be found that night. Another thing which
can always be understood is money values. Between these two things
we managed finally to hire a boat for thirty coppers to land us in the

village. It was one of the small dirty river boats with some ten filthy members of a family living within, but it looked like a motor launch to us.

They did not land us in the village, but on the main canal dyke. We searched our jeans for the necessary coppers but could find only twelve. The only other money we had was a dollar. Finally, Long One located an American nickel which he carried around as a lucky piece. They probably thought in the darkness that it was a Chinese cent piece and were satisfied. So were we, for a nickel is really worth about twelve coppers Chinese money, and we knew that they would treasure it far beyond that.

As we walked along the high embankment towards the dim lights of the village we perceived that our troubles were not yet solved. There seemed no possible way for us to recognize our boat among the hundred similar ones on the river bank. We had a flag to be sure, but it was too dark even to see it against the skyline. We began to shout out as we walked along, mingling our Chinese mouthy vowels with the hoarse shouts of those on the boats, for a Chinese boat colony is always a babel of sounds, no one apparently heeding the remarks of the others. "Is that a foreign boat?" we cried: "Is that an American boat?" "Have you seen a foreign boat?" Evidently no one had.

Finally, we stopped at the little open shop of a candle and tobacco store for a consultation. There came a man who spoke in English and who was proud to display it, telling us that six foreigners had passed through the village, so we at least knew that we were on the right track. We bought a paper lantern and candle for four coppers to light our way over the mud of the lower river bank, a bag of peanuts to relieve the sharpness of our hunger, and started again on our search.

Not a boat would heed our calls and we reached the end of the long line without success. Long One fired his gun, but that was useless, for firecrackers are always going off in China and no one would recognize a gunshot. As a last resort we decided to try one other boat whose light at the masthead could just be seen in the distance down the canal. As we approached it we looked anxiously at the mast-head, and behold! the Stars and Stripes were flashing in the light of the lantern. We were home!

Life on a Chinese river boat for eight men, two dogs, merchants and crew, might be termed a crowded existence. Our one living room was soon so jammed with guns, clothing, boots, and other possessions that when one wanted anything he almost had to dig it out. And when you wished to move, it meant a general shifting as though playing checkers. The dogs occupied the choice floor space near the stove which, by the way, worked pretty well when the pipe was not choked up or falling down. The table shifted about in accordance with the time of day, being in the center at meal time to hold the main essentials in eating utensils. Guns and cameras were in each corner. Trunks and suitcases served as chairs. Clothes were hung all around the walls and helped keep out the air which the paper windows let in. But fortunately we were leading the simple life and were easily satisfied. One basin served as wash bowl for the bunch, one towel also; a change of underclothes was a bath (except when Yankee fell in a canal); and no one shaved. We ate ravenously, for the days of walking in the open air made us hungry as the proverbial bears, and the chow was hearty.

As I was writing these lines, I was interrupted by cries of alarm from the cook. The boat had tipped as the breeze caught our great square sail, and the oil stove had overflowed and blazed high. Prime Mover came to the rescue and soon put it out.

But as I was saying, the chow has been fine. Chinese are fine cooks and we have had such things as potatoes, rice, hot biscuits, meat pie, and our own game (pheasant, duck, rabbit and pigeon), and the usual goods which can be brought along. We sleep splendidly too; most of us on camp cots covered with Chinese "phoo-khe's" (a thin mattress) and in improvised sleeping bags. When not hunting or eating we spend our time reading, playing cards or swapping yarns.

February 11, 1918

This is the greatest day in the Chinese calendar, the time in China when our Christmas, Easter, 4[th.] of July and Washington's Birthday are rolled into one: the first day of the Chinese New Year.

We were up before daybreak, and even at that early hour there was evidence of festivity. Every boat on the canal had a tiny Christmas tree in front, was liberally plastered with red paper and new pictures of gods, and had floating from the masthead a huge red flag. Firecrackers were still going off, the remnant of a terrific bombardment at midnight. Occasionally also there was a great ringing of gongs, accompanied by a fusillade of small crackers, a terrifying sound to one unaccustomed to the mild nature of the Chinese. As we walked along the canal embankment with its row of thatched cottages we were greeted by wide smiles and a hearty New Year wish from the natives who were clad in bright blue gowns, starchy in their newness. "*Koong-kyi, koong-kyi*" they said; and we replied "*Koong-kyi, fah-tse*" (Happy New Year to you).

The canal at this point was beautiful. It ran between two high banks, one of them the tow path and the other crowned with a row of old willows. On the other side of the willows there was a great shallow lake with patches of reeds stretching as far as the eye could reach into the mists of the early morning. And on the tow path side the country was lower than the level of water in the canal and was also interspersed with shallow lakes and canals. Where the sun was rising there were villages and plowed fields and grave mounds.

We were looking for ducks and we found them in one of the larger ponds just outside the canal, but they were too far out to get up. We waited around until the sun was high above the trees and then went on down the canal. We had a beautiful walk. Both the people and the land seemed to be happy on this holiday morning.

Once we saw what we thought were geese on a pond across the canal. Three of us crossed over by stopping a passing boat and made wide detours to surround the pond. I crawled for fifty yards in the mud to get a shot, for geese are rare birds. We got them, three of them, and they were sea gulls!

Then we put off through the open country, taking an occasional shot at pigeons but chiefly enjoying the New Year sights in the many villages. Every house was decorated with red and had round splotches of white powder spread in regular patterns over the front yard and the hard packed mud floor of the interior. The people all wore new clothes, the children particularly being bedecked in bright shades of red and blue. Not a man or a woman was working and we proved the chief attraction of their idle hours. They followed us in droves, children yelling, dogs barking; they showed us pigeons and woodpeckers; marveled at our guns, scrambled for our shells as we ejected them. Once we hired a boat to cross a small canal, but before the farmer would unlock the padlock, break the skin ice and ferry us across, he insisted upon burning some incense and paper money and firing a salvo of crackers.

We found our ship, with tiffin ready, awaiting us at a village called Rojen. That afternoon the Long One and I went scouting in the neighboring country. We did not expect to find game and did not care much, for it was a beautiful day and it was fun merely to walk along the canals, stroll through the villages, and rest in the warm pockets between grave mounds. But as is usual when hunting, the game was where we least expected to find it. In a chain of ponds, close under the main canal dyke, we ran across two flocks of ducks. And with the help of a group of Chinese youngsters as retrievers, between us we bagged five teal and a Hell-diver.

February 12, 1918

Today we went off on a long hunt inland for pheasant. We traveled in a small punt down a side canal. One of our boatman was cross-eyed and he brought us bad luck. A whole morning's scouting through a reed covered marsh, where there should have been birds aplenty, did not bring us a single pheasant. So in the afternoon we kept on up the Grand Canal, landing occasionally to shoot pigeon in the willows on the bank and try for pheasant in likely looking clumps of reeds. Here the Long One got a beautiful cock pheasant.

At one village we were walking along the banks of the canals with half the town out watching us, when suddenly the whole of our audience broke into howls of laughter. We looked around for the cause of their merriment and saw three women running for all they were worth across the flat country away from our side of the canal. They had been approaching the dyke when we foreign devils came along with our guns and dogs. The last we saw of them they were still running and the village was still laughing.

February 13, 1918

Last night the Long One tried sleeping on deck. After midnight it started to rain. He would have been all right even then, but one of the crew was solicitous about his health and awoke him. As soon as he had stumbled in and set up his cot, the rain ceased.

In the morning we found ourselves tied up just outside the walls of a city by the name of Kau Yui. It was a filthy place outside the walls, for in all Chinese cities the beggars and the very poor have their mud huts strung along outside, where land is cheaper and there is no protection from robbers. But when we had gone within the city gate and climbed a nearby pagoda we saw that it was a most interesting city. The pagoda itself was a rather unusual one, being square in shape and rather Romanesque in design. After climbing its seven flights of broken down steps we had a magnificent view of all the neighboring country. The city spread out far to one side, a mass of tiled roofs and leafless trees of a beautiful silvery gray shade, broken in spots by the sweeping lines of temple roofs and the abrupt upstanding pagodas. The battlemented wall marked the limits of the city and just outside it ran the Grand Canal, recognizable by the succession of sails flitting smoothly along. And outside this canal was a lake, a great sheet of water stretching away to the horizon and dotted with square sails.

Kau Yui Pagoda

129

We spotted an interesting looking temple and made for it. As we walked through the streets, one of them actually wide enough for an automobile, it was evident that few foreigners had been in this city before, for we attracted great attention. By the time we had inquired for and found the Post Office, we had gathered an interested audience to watch us write postals home. The Postmaster was very much confused by the huge trade we brought him. He could hardly make change in his eagerness but was volubly assisted by all the onlookers, who pressed against us four deep. Then came the daughter of the house, who had been to a Mission School and knew a little English. "Do you know Miss King?" she asked. We disclaimed acquaintance. "She lives in America," gave us no further clue, and even the elucidating remark that she lived in New York, did not help much. Yankee asked her whether any foreigners lived in the city, any Americans. "I live in this house" she replied. "Where did you go to school?" brought the response "My name is Tsung-yoen." Finally we had to forgo this interesting conversation, and after her father Postmaster had served us tea, we went forth in search of further adventure.

We found a temple where the two storied pagoda at the entrance gate straddled the narrow street. It was a most interesting place, consisting of a succession of temple courtyards and temple rooms, each with its tables of sacred vessels and its hideous gods. Most of the main idols, however, were hidden by a screen. After we passed through a seemingly endless line of these temples and corridors, we came to the last one, the head idol's dwelling place. Here a dirty priest offered us a seat and brought us still dirtier tea with a red berry within. We had to drink it to be polite and also we had to make an offering of a few coppers for their hospitality.

By this time, the crowd that had followed us from the post office gathered many recruits in this temple and as we went down its long corridors they made quite a procession. They were a cheerful bunch, joking, and laughing and treating us as interesting specimens of some strange animals. If we retreated with any speed they made jeering sounds like a pack of hounds after a retreating boar. We were interested to know how many there were, so I acted as decoy and walked ahead while the Long One and Yankee hid on each side of a doorway and took a census. There were sixty-seven.

Like a circus parade we now made our way through the city streets, people staring, dogs barking, children yelling. Even when we reached the city gate with its rounded flanking wall they followed us without. And as we crossed the moat and made our way across the ploughed fields we could see the group in their bright blue gowns waving us farewell. The moat, the battlemented walls, the rounded buttresses of the gate, made a scene typically Medieval in character, as is so often the case in China.

For the next two days we hunted around the city of Kau Yui. Off toward the lake there was a great expanse of semi-marshy land, intersected by canals and abounding in patches of reeds. We went out in small boats, carrying along some of our crew to act as beaters. They would go into the patches of reeds, yelling and beating the grass, while we placed ourselves outside with our guns ready, waiting for the pheasants. And four times out of five they would scare out several pheasant. We would hear a whirr of wings and a gold and green streak would go by. They were hard to hit and we often missed, so the birds had an even chance, in spite of the fact that we were using the rather unsportsman-like method of beaters. In two hunts the party shot about sixteen pheasant.

Boat Family

131

One afternoon we had an experience with Chinese boat people which gave us an insight into their manner of life. We had hired one of the many small river boats, which thronged the waters about the city wall, to take us across country to the neighboring lake for ducks. The boat was about twenty feet long and four wide, square at the ends, flat bottomed and divided into three sections by board partitions. Needless to say also it was dirty. Over the middle section there was a rounded cover of straw matting, in front were two oars, and in the rear compartment was an oar, a rudder, and an earthenware bowl containing an iron pot which served as a stove. In this humble home there lived a flourishing family: a dull-looking father clad in filthy rags, the mother with a stolid face but unusually good features, who wore garments and trousers so much padded that she resembled a great bear, a little girl whose eyes made her almost beautiful and whose method of hair dressing and general air of self-confidence gave one the impression she was fully grown, also a little boy with some fine eyes and a very old grandfather with slanting eyebrows and upturned mouth corners, and a baby so padded with rags that he could sleep standing up, which was a fortunate thing for when we were occupying the middle section there was no room for him to lie down. And in a twenty foot punt this family lived and were happy, at least I am sure the children were.

We lived with them for two afternoons, for twice they took us on long vain hunts for duck. The mother rowed in the stern, the father in the bow, the little boy and girl took turns at the front oar and the rudder. Each day it was dark by the time we started home, for the ducks did not fly until twilight. Even then it proved too dark to shoot them. We could hear the flocks go by over head with a great swish of wings like falling water, but only occasionally could we catch their outlines against the evening sky.

It was a cold three-hour trip home through the canals. Fortunately, we had an acetylene hunting lamp but even then we were never sure of being on the correct waterway. To keep warm, we took turns at the oars and when we reached the Grand Canal we got out the tow line, hitched ourselves up with the ragged boatman and pulled the little boat two miles home to our warm ship and supper.

And there we left the little family to the cold, and the mother to make a fire in her bowl with the dry sticks which littered the floor, and cook the evening rice. And then they would pull out their worn quilt and retire for the night.

Once during the trip, we lost the father's cloth belt while towing on the canal. We paid him for it, but the next morning we found out that in spite of the lateness of the hour and the fact that he had been rowing all the afternoon and evening, he had gone back to look for his dirty strip of cloth. Thus close to the minimum do they live and yet they burned incense and the little girl had earrings.

February 15, 1918

The Grand Canal shows evidence in spots of being a great engineering achievement. The dykes for example are splendidly constructed. Some day they will make an ideal railway embankment or perhaps a highway which will connect Peking and Shanghai. On the wide top of the main right hand dyke there is room for both railway and road. This embankment is pierced in places to allow the water in the canal to flow into the low-lying country. These spillways are solidly built of granite. In two places we found spillways some hundred yards apart and between them ran roads built of granite blocks smooth as a ballroom floor.

Today we started home, our allotted time being nearly up. The current was now with us and also we had a favoring wind, so we made splendid time, going over in two days and nights the territory it had taken us five days to cover coming up. We hunted as we went and the very last day had splendid luck, beating up pheasant and rabbit and some rare mandarin ducks.

We took stock of our hunting and our bodily conditions. Of the latter the least said the better, for although we were hard from our exercise and days in the open, we were filthy after no baths for a week and every man with a budding mustache and beard. Story Teller looked a tramp, with a black growth all over his face; Newly-Wed was planning how he could slip home without being seen by wifey and Prime Mover had sprouted in splotches with a hideous red beard.

The census of our hunting was more pleasant. It was rather unevenly divided, the big lots falling to Old Hand, Southernman, and

Story Teller, but we were all satisfied. We had 47 pheasant, 25 teal, 4 ducks, 5 rabbits, 100 pigeons, and a number of smaller worthless birds.

At Yangchow we parted with Prime Mover, the stove and chow, at Chinkiang the rest of the party split up, we paid off the river boat, and the railroad bore us back to showers and baths, clean linen and newspapers.

Farmers Along the Grand Canal

Flooding a Rice Field

Threshing Rice

Watering Cans

Rich Mud

January 1, 1918
Last Days in the East

The day after New Years from the front verandah of this Middle School building I have just witnessed a scene typical to Chinese students and of the colorful Orient. St. John's today won first place in a great Oratorical Contest in Shanghai open to all China and the students were celebrating the event. As usual there were firecrackers — no Chinese event, be it wedding, funeral, or christening would be complete without them — and they were there in unusual quantities. The air was alive with the bursting bombs. Not content with placing them on the ground or even with holding them in the hand, the students were lighting them and throwing them wildly into the air, so that when the first explosion took place, it was a gamble where the firecracker would be driven for its second and greater explosion. The whole triangle was a miniature battlefield with red glare, shouts and yells, smoke, and explosions.

Meanwhile down the road, hastened along by the martial sounds of a bugle and a kettle drum, there came a great column of gowned figures. The leaders carried the banner announcing the victory, the whole front of the column was alive with Chinese lanterns swinging on the ends of long poles, and the students themselves were singing and cheering. The dark column, headed by its picturesque lights, wound like some great oriental dragon across the Compound; it disappeared behind the Library; the firecrackers ceased; and gradually there succeeded the normal peace of a Compound night, broken only by the watchman's bamboo rattle as he made his rounds.

January 20, 1918

We are given occasional instances in our work here at St. John's of how closely bound by superstition and tradition are even the most highly educated "modern" Chinese. A student with whom I often have long conversations (the son of the former Minister to Belgium, whom I have previously mentioned) just came into my study to give me his absence slip for a six-day leave. We are on the verge of examinations and so I asked him why he was going home at this important time. He answered, without showing any particular signs of sorrow, that he was going home for his father's funeral. I recalled instantly that his father had been dead as long as I had known him so I inquired further.

It turned out that this was the third commemoration of his father's decease, and certain ceremonies in which the eldest son played the leading part made it essential that he be present. Further questioning revealed the fact that the ceremonies were being performed at this particular time because a soothsayer had so decreed. Any other time would bring bad luck on the deceased and his spirit could not rest in peace. Much money had been paid the soothsayer to decide this important matter. He did not believe in all this he said and he smiled broadly as he said it. "No, no; he did not believe in soothsayers."

I pressed him as to why he observed such customs if he did not believe in them. Well, he had no say in the matter. His uncle was head of the family. His uncle did not believe in it either. He was an educated man. He did it because it was custom. For a thousand years this had been done.

"Yes, it does interfere with work," he said and it was indeed rather silly for an educated man to be thus dependent upon money-loving soothsayers.

"Why don't you take a stand against it?" I asked

Horrible thought!

"If anything happened to the family, everybody would say it was my fault. Besides it had been done for a thousand years!"

And thus our conversation continued; he acknowledging that many such customs and beliefs were absurd, but being so close bound by the overwhelming traditions of his ancestors, he did not dare change one whit of the beliefs which he did not really believe. He looked in a frightened manner over his shoulder as he made some of his ad-missions, and when I pressed him regarding his belief in soothsayers he acknowledged that he really did believe that they could foretell the future, could find lost articles, etc. He cited instances, and when I told him of the "law of chance" and used the Greek oracles as an example, he could not see the force of my argument.

It happens that I had a valuable watch stolen last Fall, and neither the watch nor the thief have ever been traced. The student knows of this and he finally gave me a challenge that he would consult a sooth-sayer, find the watch, and thus prove the efficacy of the said gentleman. I did not object in the least, and so it has been agreed that while he is home on this six day's leave he is to consult a good soothsayer regarding my watch and if possible even find the thief.

June 29 - August 1, 1918, outbound

The journey home from China began at the end of one of Shanghai's hot June days. It was a day of feverish activity, a final trip to the city regarding tickets and money, a last packing of trunks and suit cases, the task of getting the baggage started on its five-mile wheelbarrow journey to the dock, the last hurried farewells to friends.

At last it was over.

The tender going to our ship was due to leave at nine. At eight on Saturday June 29th, we actually started the journey, the seven bachelors of our Mess going in town by automobile. We passed through the Chinese village of Zou Ka Doo, where the half-naked population crowded the narrow road, and the smelly, noisy, open shops buzzed with their trade. It was my last touch of pure China: of the dirt and smells, the noisy jabber and activity, the spiky heads, or filthy queues, the blue cotton garments, the ragged beggars and coolies, the shine of naked yellow bodies.

Then we had honked free of the noise and light and were on the winding Bubbling Well Road, bounded with the well built homes of foreigners. Then into the glare and showiness of the Chinese section of Shanghai's main business street resplendent with electric lights and gaudy signs and crowded with rickshaws, automobiles, and richly dressed Chinese, the traffic guided by huge Sikhs in red turbans with their carbines on their backs. Finally, through the foreign section of the street, now dark and quiet, for the "outside country men" close their shops early in this hot weather, and on to the Bund with its succession of splendid office buildings resembling a real foreign city.

The tender left from the Custom Jetty of the Bund and the jetty was well filled with our friends down to see us off. We steamed out into the river at nine amid shouting farewells and waving handkerchiefs.

Three miles down the Whangpoo our ship, the *Kashima Maru* of Nippon Yusen Kaisha line, was moored. We were agreeably surprised at her size. As the tender circled about her to the steps going up her side, she towered far above us and looked most impressive. Our cabin was No. 17, Roberts, Norton and myself being together. It was fairly large and very well fitted up. At three the next morning our journey actually started.

After daybreak, as I lay in the upper berth I could see the green flat banks of the Whangpoo slipping by. Presently they gave way to a wide expanse of yellow water with a dim shoreline which indicated we were in the Yangtze. Then we passed fleets of junks with their great square sails and flat ends, and by breakfast time the shore was out of sight and we had said goodbye to China. Finally, even the yellow water of the Yangtze gave way to the green of the sea and the ship began to rise and fall to the ground swell of the Yellow Sea.

July 1, 1918

Why this is called the Yellow Sea I do not know. True it is yellow enough in great semicircles at the mouths of the Yangtze and the Yellow Rivers, but the sea itself is as blue as the Pacific. It has a reputation for roughness, being shallow and subject to typhoons. However, this is the fourth time I have crossed it and the only time when it has been at all rough. Quite a breeze kicked up when we were well outside the Yangtze, and the ship began to pitch and toss. By tiffin time there were white caps and a row of figures prostrate in streamer chairs on the deck. In the afternoon it was worse and but few showed up for dinner. Norton was the first to succumb but was followed rapidly by both Roberts and MacNair, and Miss Fullerton. I felt a bit odd but always better after eating.

The boat is a very good one. I am agreeably surprised by its size and cleanliness. There is a wide promenade deck, very pretty dining room, social room and smoking room, and the cabins are fairly large and well outfitted.

Service is good too, though Japanese boys are not as thoughtful as are Chinese. They are very polite, but give you the impression of having their pleasant smiles and suave words on tap. The ship is about 19,000 tons and gives you the impression of being very long, but the accommodations for passengers are restricted pretty well amidships, there being extra-large cargo space and hatchways in the bow. The masts are particularly strong and derricks are abundant. I can foresee much loading in Japanese ports. We are lightly laden now and for that reason are rolling more.

Yesterday the breeze was so fresh that white clothes disappeared and rugs were acceptable. But this afternoon (the second day out) with Japan in sight, it is becoming muggy again. We have spent our time lazily, sleeping, eating and reading.

July 2, 1918

The beautiful outer harbor of Nagasaki, with its boundary of wooded hills came in sight early in the afternoon. We anchored and were there most of the remainder of the day, broiling in the hot sun, while the Japanese doctors and inspectors performed their duties. They are most particular in wartime and examined every person on the boat, asking various questions about ancestors, destinations, and occupation. My ancestors for some generations back having been American, I had no trouble and was readily granted a pass to go ashore!

There was an American transport in the harbor and it disgorged a mass of khaki figures just before our launch landed us at the jetty. As a result, we found the little Japanese streets alive with American faces and voices. Japan is distinctly different from China, and to those of us who have lived in the latter country it is not as pleasing as for one just out from home, for whom it is a novelty. The streets are of course cleaner than they are in China, but there is a disagreeable odor of sour sake about them. At least this is true of Nagasaki, for it caters to the seafaring man, who longs for a drink and for women. It is therefore a cheap city and a rotten one.

We wandered about the gravelled streets, looking at the open shops and stopping now and then to price or buy. In almost every store they spoke broken English. They are outwardly most polite to the purchaser; one old lady fanned us as she sold us postcards. The streets abound in kimono-clad figures shuffling along in their clogs or with half naked coolies or hand carts drawn by decrepit horses. Occasionally there are bulls laden with merchandise. The shuffle of sandals and the shrill whistle of blind men are the distinctive sounds.

Our party split after wandering a bit, and four of us had dinner in a restaurant above the railway station, where we could see through the open window to the beautiful harbor in its amphitheatre of terraced hills and the ships waiting to go out. Then we wandered about again until launch time. It was hot and the streets were crowded. There were many little booths where shaved ice, flavored with various deadly looking concoctions, were sold. This is the Japanese equivalent of ice cream and they love it. Again we noticed the Japanese propensity for a lack of our Western sense of modesty, for families were going to bed in full view of the street.

Coaling

143

There were many American soldiers about, some of them already drunk. We questioned some and found they were of the regular army just out from the States. For three weeks they had been on the Pacific, 700 of them cooped up in the small transport, badly fed and bored with life. This was their first stop since Honolulu. Small wonder they were making the most of it. One man to whom I talked was from Pennsylvania, near Harrisburg. He had wanted to go to France but now found himself enroute to the Phillipines. He was homesick, I could see, and tired of army life already.

Night on a steamer in a Japanese port in Summer is no fun, for the heat in the cabins is terrific and particularly when the ship is coaling We were also loading — barges full of shouting coolies on both sides, ladders up the ship filled with women handing up baskets of coal, derricks and donkey engines rattling, the air choking with coal dust, the decks filthy with the same. It continued all night and into the morning. But all things have an end and so by noon they began to give the ship a bath and we steamed out of the beautiful harbor into a cool, clean rain outside.

July 4, 1918, enroute through Japan by rail

Inland Sea

144

All that afternoon we followed the beautiful coast line northward toward the straits of Shimonoseki, with constantly changing scenery and a varied assortment of passing vessels. A delightful night on quiet seas carried us through the Straits and well into the Inland Sea, so that by the time we got up in the morning we were in the midst of the most wonderful part. We stood in the bow before breakfast, while the ship went through the famous Geiho Strait, smooth, clean, green water in curious whirlpools and eddies, precipitous rocky banks well wooded and green covered, a white lighthouse, square rigged fishing junks, a scene hard to rival in the world. All that morning it was almost equally beautiful, though constantly varying. There were beautiful little rocky islands, others entirely covered with a close crop of green, the shore in places was wild and uncivilized, in others the hillsides were terraced for rice fields or rose in checkerboard pattern, and little tiled villages nestled at the foot. The water was smooth as a lake but in places there was a swift current which eddied against the rocks. There were many boats, most of them junks but some few were schooner-rigged and reminded me of home.

Geiho Strait

After tiffin, the sea broadened out and late in the afternoon we came in sight of the smokestacks and shipping of Kobe. Again we went through the force of doctor's and police inspection and again were delayed by Japanese official red tape, so much so this time that it

145

was three hours before the ship finally warped in behind the new break-water and the launch left for shore. It was rough despite the breakwater and a number of people were sick as the small boat bobbed up and down beside the ship. But we finally got ashore and rushed our bags through the customs by getting there first and declaring that we had no tobacco. Then Roberts, Campbell and I boarded a tram for the station, being crowded in on the rear platform with a mass of perspiring Japanese. The conductor could speak no English but we managed to give him our fare and by good luck landed at the railroad station. Japanese stations impress one as dirty and nondescript, but in this respect they resemble stations the world over. Also they are smelly, chiefly with Japanese tobacco, and resound with the scrape of clogs on stone. But the porters are excellent and there is generally an Inquiry office where someone speaks English, so a foreigner has little difficulty in travelling. We were going to Tokyo, but found there was no express until late in the evening, so after wandering about the streets for an hour or so we returned and were fortunate in getting the last three upper berths on the train.

Then began a long journey northward. The trains in Japan are narrow gauge and not overly tall, so the berths are not all they might be. I could not stretch out and had no air, but survived the night without a grouch in the morning. We were on the train until after tiffin.

It was beautiful country through which we passed: great stretches of rice paddy fields under water with the green shoots just coming up, wooded hillsides, neat little villages, thatched cottages in the country, numerous streams, bridges, and water wheels, glimpses of the sea and of the mountains. Part of the time we climbed steadily until it was quite cool and misty; this was at the foot of Fuji, which we could not see because of the mist. Then we went down to the hot lowland again and by the time we had passed through Yokohama and arrived at Central Station, Tokyo, it was a hot Summer afternoon.

I have been in Tokyo four times and each time it has been miserably hot. This time there was a strong breeze, but it only served to kick up the white dust with which all the streets were liberally supplied.

After arrangements with the rickshaw office in the station we rolled in the high, baby carriages down Tokyo's chief street toward the

146

other station. There were many fine buildings most of them low and Japanese in style. The street was broad and a double track tram ran through the center. I noticed many new buildings and some steel ones just going up. Japan is evidently prospering by the war. Incidentally, I tried in almost every department or clothing store to buy a pair of socks and could not buy a pair large enough.

At the Veno Station we took a train again, this time bound for Nikko. Part way up we ran into a terrific thunderstorm but arrived safely late in the evening and are now at the Konaya Hotel. This is July 4th. and I saw one lonely American flag in Tokyo.

July 5, 1918, Nikko

The Japanese have a proverb: Do not say "magnificent" until you have seen Nikko, and like most proverbs it is eminently true. Two previous trips through Japan had rather cured me of temple seeing, but I have revised my opinion of temples since coming here. The mountainous district in which the little Japanese village and the two foreign hotels are located is studded with the most marvelous creations of red lacquer, carved wood, gilt and gold of which it is possible to conceive. The two series of gateways and temples which have made Nikko famous would alone pay for the visit up, were it not also that the setting for them cannot be surpassed. They are approached by winding stone stairs, leading up through avenues of giant cryptomeria to an immense height and join overhead in the most delicate of leafy roofs. No cathedral aisle on earth could approach the magnificence of this avenue. There is a sense of vastness about it, of solidity and strength combined with delicacy and beauty. The temples themselves, rising tier on tier on the mountain side, are each set in an amphitheatre of the same giant trees, filling in so well that the whole seems the work of nature struggling toward perfection.

We saw the temples under conditions which accentuate the atmosphere of the East. There was misty rain which made the vastness more vast, softened the brilliant red and gold, and added picturesqueness to the Japanese pilgrims trailing to pay their respects at the shrines.

We spent the whole morning seeing the temples and tombs, wandering about through the rain with our paper umbrellas (bought on emergency for 70 sen), removing our shoes at each entrance, gaping and struggling for descriptive words at the magnificence of it all. In the afternoon it still rained, so except for a shopping trip to the hundreds of curio shops which constitute the village street, we remained indoors. Japan hotel life in the rain is a dreary existence for passing travelers, but we enjoyed the change of food from the ship, and the mountain air was most refreshing after a year in the low-lying mud flats of Shanghai.

July 6, 1918, Yokohama

"Mirabile dictu" it cleared up during the night, so before the giggling little maid had brought us our shaving water we were up and dressed in old clothes. We planned a visit to Lake Chuzenji, some nine miles in the mountains above Nikko. The first stage was on a tiny crowded Japanese tram, so crowded that we had to stand and so tiny that by standing we could not see out of the windows and hence missed some very fine scenery as the electric car crawled up the valley. At the terminal we began to walk, a walk which speedily became a climb. The road wound steeply up the mountain but we were able to take short cuts straight up through the woods. The air became clearer as we advanced, the sunlight glanced through the trees, and it was a splendid walk. At intervals there were little tea houses where one could rest and drink from the tiny handle-less cups while overlooking the valley below.

After about an hour's climbing we reached a magnificent waterfall, known as the Kegon Falls. The surplus water from Lake Chuzenji above tumbled in a mountain torrent for some hundred yards, and then plunged out over the lip of a rocky precipice and down into a natural amphitheatre 250 feet below, a setting which seemed planned.

Lake Chuzenji itself is a body of clear green water on top of the mountain and itself is surrounded by mountains covered with trees to their summits. There was an atmosphere of peace and quiet about the lake and its surroundings which one could feel on first reaching its shore.

We were there only long enough for a row across to a bronze Torii on the shore, and then had to start back in order to catch a train. By hard walking we just caught the tram and were back at our hotel for tiffin.

In the afternoon we took tram again for Yokohama. Japanese train service seems as a rule to be excellent; trains on time, officials courteous, and things fairly clean. One great convenience is the method of eating. If there is no foreign diner (only the big express trains have them) it is possible to buy a neat little box of hot rice and a similar box of meat and vegetables, a pair of chopsticks, and a tiny earthenware pot of tea and cup. This whole meal costs only twenty-four sen (12 cents gold) and is really excellent, giving one quite enough. Once I had a pot of hot rice and eels which was very, very good.

Back in Tokyo we were obliged to cross the city again by rickshaw. There are taxis now (Fords, of course) but they are scarce. Rickshaws in Japan are very expensive and the rickshaw men, while neater and cleaner than those in China, are very slow and apt to be insolent in the ports. Arrangements as to fare must be made beforehand and even then they are bound to kick for more at the end.

The New Central station in Tokyo is most impressive. It is a tremendously long red and white brick building containing a hotel as well as station. From it we caught an electric train for Yokohama, which went part way on the elevated. Looking down into the little Japanese homes with the families sitting about on the floor, or about their low tables at dinner, and stopping suddenly at the many stations we were reminded of the New York elevated. But that was only because we had not been home for years. To a New Yorker the scenes would have been far from natural.

At Yokohama we took a Ford taxi to the Pleasanton Hotel. It was hot in Yokohama and the smell of the harbor and streets after the clear air of the mountains was most unpleasant. Then too there were mosquitoes and dance music next door which continued far into the night.

July 7, 1918, Kamakura

The foreigners in Yokohama live on a plateau above the native city which is known as "The Bluff." Here they have their foreign homes (very ugly, in comparison to Japan's artistic sensibilities) as well as churches and theatres, and even their own burial ground.

We soon tired of Yokohama, the ports are spoiled by the foreign residents, being neither truly Japanese nor truly foreign, so we took train for an hour to the small town of Kamakura. Here, in spite of our ignorance of the language, we ventured to try a Japanese Inn. With the aid of the phrases in our guide book we managed to make the old lady and her husband at the door understand that we wished a room for two days and Japanese chow. He in turn told us it would be 3 Y each per man per day. So we removed our shoes and were shown through the slippery corridors to a bare little room with shutters of papers which left two sides open to the world and from which we could see the sea almost below us. We went in bathing almost immediately and again were thrown with the Japanese in that close way which we Westerners consider so immodest. Coming out of the sea for example and into the bath room of the Inn we found there was a Japanese woman inside without a stitch calmly taking a bath. And in the same room were two Japanese men doing the same, and a foreigner sitting calmly in the tub. They think nothing of this at all. Sometimes it would be better if we dropped our false modesty and were more like them.

We wound up the day by seeing the famed Diabutsu, that great bronze image of the Buddha with the sleepy eyes and air of contemplation. It is expressive of the East and a wonderful idol, yet in many ways I was disappointed. It was smaller than I had imagined, the mouth is tremendously weak, and the setting is not at all impressive. The joints in the bronze sheets also show and the metal is very much stained with the weather. I always had the impression it was solid, where as it is but a hollow shell and one can climb within.

July 8, 1918, hotel life

Life in a Japanese Inn has its advantages, its drawbacks and its humorous side. The chief source of the last element are the little maids who constantly hang around and are always ready with their giggles and jokes. The advantages are the absolute freedom from convention and the simplicity of life. You do not care what clothes you have on and can wander about with perfect propriety in as few as you wish.

150

I shaved this morning beside a young lady who was performing her morning ablutions, both of us stripped to the waist. Then too in our little room on the second floor, open to the sea and the world in general we are not troubled with chairs but sit about on cushions. When meal time comes it is brought to us and placed on a low table in the middle of the room. At night, quilts are spread on the floor and lo, we are ready for bed.

The disadvantages arise chiefly from our ignorance of the language and our lack of acquaintance with customs. The food for example is poor, because they try to give us an attempt at foreign chow and we cannot tell them that what we want is pure Japanese food. Sitting on the floor gets terribly wearisome too and we long for chairs. But the greatest discomfort is at night, for they insist upon closing tight the outside shutters of the house. We insisted upon having at least one shutter open for air and there ensued a duel, we would be just asleep and a maid would come and shut them up. Out of our quilts we would jump and make her open them. Half an hour later this would be repeated. Finally, a coolie came and brought a grating which he fixed in place of the shutter. We accepted the compromise, thanked him and went to sleep. Half an hour later we were awake with mosquitoes, and for the rest of the night we fought them and vowed we would have a net for the next night.

We saw the Buddha again in the morning and I was more impressed than at first. The great image grows upon one. There is an air of mystery about the droopy eyes and downcast mien which seems to defy solution.

Another bath in the sea followed and then, after a wretched Japanese tiffin of cold rice, fish and omelette, we took a tram for a half hour's ride along the coast to the island of Enoshima. This is a rocky isle just off the coast and connected to it by a rickety wooden causeway. The whole island is covered with shrines and paths and stone steps, but it is spoiled by the many trinket shops. The most interesting thing was a cave which extended about a hundred yards in the rock at sea level, gradually narrowing to a point.

July 10, 1918, Yokohama

Our ship was not as yet in port, having been many days in Kobe loading and having two other stops on the way up. All the next day (today) we were in port. We had been due to sail at three in the afternoon, but the great pile of bags and of beans and boxes of merchandise which littered the warehouse could not be got on board and the date of sailing was delayed a day. All night and all day the cranes and derricks worked and the ship lay in the broiling sun. A brisk breeze and the sight of Fuji with a broad collar of clouds helped make it endurable. Also Yokohama is a great center for curios, damascene, and silk.

There are few signs of war activity in Japan. In fact, the one thing which suggested war in our stay was the sound of big guns in the distance during our stay at Kamakura. As I write, the ship resounds the activities which precede departure. All morning the loading of boxes and coal has been feverish and now with the time of leaving only three quarters of an hour away the derrick is still working and the air is filled with coal dust. We are so laden that the waterline has risen perceptibly. This should at least prevent rolling in heavy weather.

New passengers have been coming on board all morning, and tiffin was quite a gala event with many Japanese in their flowery gowns or in uniform and gold lace. And now final farewells are being said.

My time in the East is short.

The excitement gradually increased as the scheduled time of leaving drew near. The last cargo to come aboard was a great pile of mail bags which were swung up the cranes in their bags of nettings. Then the whistle sounded and the gongs beat. Those who had come on board to say goodbye began hurriedly to leave over the high gangplank, adding the gay colors of Japanese clothing and the white of the foreigners to the ugly gray of the wharf.

A final whistle as the ship's bell stuck six, and the straining coolies pushed away the gangplank and began to cast off the hawsers.

There is an emotional thrill in all leave-taking and it is particularly keen when a big ship puts off. In our case, too, we were going home — most of us after years in the Orient. And when ones goes home in wartime, it is to unknown conditions and an unknown future.

The crowd on the ship cracked jokes and made light of it as people always do when they really feel a thrill. They broke jokingly into "Over There" as we warped away from the dock, but they really meant it: "The Yanks are coming, the Yanks are coming; and we won't be back until it's over over there."

There was cheering on the dock and the usual waving of hats and handkerchiefs. A puffing tug pulled our bow around until we headed out between the red and white lighthouses which mark the breakwater of Yokohama harbor. And we steamed slowly out and into the blue green water and whitecaps of the Pacific.

It had been 96 degrees in the shade in Yokohama, out in the harbor there was a splendid, cool breeze. The sky-line was piled up with fleecy white clouds and so we could not see Fuji to say goodbye.

We were sorry for that, for there is a superstition that unless one can say goodbye to Fuji as he leaves Yokohama harbor, he is not coming back to the East.

END

Epilogue

L ife on shipboard on the homeward passage assumed a routine, each day like the other. After two weeks at sea they sighted land and soon arrived in Vancouver where Arch boarded a train and began the long cross-country trip home.

America was a great exotic thrill for him — the large size of everything compared to China, the vast spaces of the Rockies, the presence of English spoken in the streets, the well-dressed people, the presence of soldiers, and also, interestingly enough, the number of black people, a welcome reminder of his childhood.

At one point on the homebound journey it came to him suddenly, as he watched the Hudson River glide by the train window, that he was seeing America as a foreigner would. He noticed the new landscapes, the luxury of even the poorer classes, the beauty and style of the women's clothes, the care with which both men and women were shod, the nasal accents, and the friendliness of everyone. These and scores of other minor things fascinated him.

Arch was held up for two days in New York City waiting for his trunks to arrive but finally, on 1st, after three years absence, he returned to Centreville.

His journals end with a single word: "Home."

Arch Mitchell left China in 1918 to join the American forces in Europe, but by the time he was ready to sail, the war was over. He went back to school and in 1922 earned a Master's Degree in English at Yale. After that, he knocked about for another two years, picking up tutoring jobs in Cambridge, Massachusetts, and at Lake Placid in the Adirondacks. Finally, unsurprisingly perhaps, he decided to join the ministry. He graduated from the Virginia Theological Seminary in 1924 and took a church in Snow Hill, Maryland, and then in Baltimore.

These were good years for him. He and his brother, John, owned a skipjack and used to take long cruises with friends on Chesapeake Bay. Arch was reportedly the most eligible bachelor in Baltimore, and it was during this period that he met a young dark-haired woman named Virginia Powers, who, after a brief courtship, he married. By that time, he was forty years old.

He accepted a teaching position at the Virginia Theological Seminary, and then, in 1931, took a job at a church in Englewood. He and Virginia had three boys, Jim, Hugh, and later in life when he was fifty, John.

When we knew him, "Pa" as we called him in his later years, seemed a somewhat world-weary, reflective man out of the long past Victorian era. He had, after all, seen a lot. He had endured the death of his parents within a month of one another, had witnessed the abject poverty of China during the Warlord period, and in the late thirties, he had gone to Europe with an international study group and traveled in Russia, and more significantly in Nazi Germany. He went to Europe as a pacifist and returned believing we had to halt the rise of Hitler, even if it meant war.

Arch grew up with positive associations with black people and his time in China only reinforced his feelings about people different than himself. He told one of his nephews after he came back from China that he would look at a person and see only another human being. Even before the Civil Rights Movement, he had integrated his all-white church in Englewood, New Jersey, much to the unease of his Wall Street parishioners. He was always politically engaged, and as a result of his liberal leanings and the fact that he had traveled in Russia, he was caught up in the accusations of the McCarthy Era. He had many supporters in the town and was well-loved, especially in the black community. Nonetheless, because of his outspoken support of civil liberties and tolerance, the accusations increased. He was the recipient of hate mail, and was known in the anti-communist press as "The Red Dean."

He retired from the church in 1963 and spent the next few years serving as interim minister and preaching at various local churches. He died in 1967 at the age of 75 and is buried in his home town of Centreville, Maryland.

His experiences in China were a major influence on his life. He maintained contact with people he had known in the East, and even years later, would still recount stories at the dinner table of his years in China, some of which, we later learned, he sanitized to protect his children.

But perhaps the most enduring legacy of his China years is his documentation of the lost world that is contained within these pages.

JAM at the Grand Canal

End Notes

Page 6

Despite their strong ancestor worship, the Chinese would stand on the graves of their forebearers and gaze with "great amazement" at the strange doings of foreign travelers. Elsewhere in his journals Arch comments that the practical Chinese grazed their animals on burial mounds. In the modern day, the old grave mounds have been swallowed by Shanghai's massive urban growth.

Page 13

Wealthy British carried overseas one of their favorite pastimes, fox hunting — only in China there were no foxes to chase, just a trail of papers to follow in a cross-country horse race.

Page 16

In late 1915, Yuan Shikai signaled that he intended to become the next Emperor of China. In a trumped-up vote of the hastily convened "Special" Representative Assembly, he was elected emperor by a vote of 1,993 to 0. But he miscalculated on the effect of this move and many of his close political allies abandoned him, shattering the solidarity of the warlord factions of the Beiyang clique.

Throughout China there were protests and marches. Yuan Shikai's prestige was diminished as province after province continued to declare independence from Peking.

In his 2003 biography, *Chiang Kai Shek: China's Generalissimo and the Nation He Lost* (Carroll & Graf, NY), Jonathan Fenby gives a detailed account of the December 5th attack on Shanghai and attributes it to discontent when Yuan proclaimed he was emperor. But Fenby also ties it to the political actions of Sun Yat-sen, the revolutionary founder of the Nationalist regime. Chiang, who later became China's Nationalist leader, was sent by Sun on a fund-raising effort to South East Asia, but determined instead to foment a revolt against Yuan Shikai Shanghai.

The plan, which partially succeeded, was to capture the Chinese cruiser *Chao Ho* in the harbor, gain the support of sailors on other Chinese navy ships, and launch a mutiny. On the evening of Sunday, December 5th, 1915, Chiang's attackers gained control of the ship, forced the sailors to man the canons and shell the Shanghai Arsenal. Eighty-five three-inch shells hit the city and eleven hit the Settlement. Significantly, they did not explode, possibly because Western business interests had sold defective munitions to the Chinese.

Cruiser Chao Ho

Other attacks were made on police stations, the telephone exchange and the electricity station, but the attackers didn't succeed in winning over the other Chinese naval ships, which began shelling the *Chao Ho*, forcing the attackers to abandon the ship and fight their way through the city.

A number of revolutionaries broke into the French compound, only to be expelled with a considerable loss of life. The Shanghai Volunteer Corps was called out. The revolt fizzled due to incompetent preparations, and Chiang escaped by hiding in a safe house in the French Concession.

Page 16

The Shanghai Volunteer Corps was a multinational volunteer militia controlled by the Shanghai Municipal Council, which governed the Shanghai International Settlement. It was initially formed in 1853 as the "British Local Volunteer Corps" and saw action in 1854 in response to threats to the compound from battling Qing and rebel forces. In 1870, it was reformed as a more vital component of the foreign military defense scheme, and was led by a British officer. Different national companies, such as the American or German, were established and trained together. It was expected that a number of young foreign businessmen and even young missionaries would serve as volunteers in the SVC.

The unit was mobilized in 1900 in response to the Boxer Uprising and again in 1914 and 1915. The British War Office supplied weapons and a commanding officer. Militia training was regular, rigorous and thorough, and Arch was proud of the fact that he moved up to the rank of Sergeant.

American Company, Shanghai Volunteer Corps, 1917, JAM at Arrow

Page 33

In 1909, a branch of the British Boys' Brigade was formed in Shanghai. It was an association of British and English-speaking Scouts, from more than forty countries, who were full-time residents of the International Settlement in Shanghai.

In 1910, twenty-five boys of several different nationalities and faiths were selected from the Boys' Brigade to establish the Shanghai Boy Scouts, forming three Troops: A, B, and C. In a year, they numbered more than forty members and six scoutmasters, who wore three different scarves. They became an independent association under the aegis of the Shanghai Municipal Council but closely linked to the Shanghai Volunteer Corps, serving as signalers or messengers. By the end of 1914, five Scouts had left to serve in the British Army as signalers.

In Shanghai, American, French, and the stateless Russian scouts were taking instructions and passing tests in English and wearing British uniforms and badges. Many had the benefit of an early British education at schools in the International Settlement, such as St. John's College.

The expedition reported on by Arch was made up of this conglomeration of Boy Scouts. The photos reveal that they wore dark uniforms with several different colored kerchiefs and had the mischievous nature of all adolescent boys. But rather than only learning camp craft and having fun, they had a real and potentially dangerous function as an extension of the Shanghai Volunteer Corps.

Page 66

This passage shows the dangers and chaos of travel in the Warlord period.

It seems reasonable that the troop train had been wrecked as a result of the recent conflict between General Chang Hsun, who had placed the boy emperor Puyi on the throne, thus briefly restoring the monarchy, and a group of generals and elite, known as the Beiyang group. The latter fought to expel General Zhang and restore the reluctant Li Yuanhong to the presidency.

Page 77

In early July 1917, the former pro-Manchu General Zhang Xun (referred to in the text as "the bandit Chang Hsun") had taken over Peking and proceeded to declare a restoration of the Qing Manchu dynasty by placing the boy emperor (poor little Puyi) on the throne. This didn't sit well with supporters of the Republic and a brief war broke out between The Army of the Republic of Duan Qirui's Northern generals and the "Pig-tail" army of Zhang Xun. The Republican Army won and threw out the last Qing monarch.

At this time China was surviving on foreign loans that were inadequate to support the government and thus the currency was debased, leading to Arch's fiscal anxiety.

Page 89

Zhang Xun, an ally of Yuan Shikai, in an attempt to sort out the complications in Peking, dissolved the provincial parliment and proclaimed the restoration of the Qing Dynasty. The revolutionaries prevailed and Chang took refuge in the Dutch Legation as his house burned.

Page 91

St. John's was an Anglican university, supported by both the British and American Episcopal World Fellowship funds. Founded in 1879, it was one of the oldest and most prestigious universities, often regarded as the Harvard of China. In 1896, the decision was made, under the leadership of Dr. Francis Hawks Pott, to become a university and at that time the school was divided into two parts: a university teaching advanced level courses, and what we now call a junior college, which retained the name St. John's College. Arch, at age twenty-four, was approved by the American Board of Missions to teach Chinese students who were still attempting to master English. He also served as what we would call today a Dormitory Master, living in the students' quarters.

Yen Hall, St. John's University

St. John's University attracted some of the brightest, most promising, and wealthiest students in China, and many of them went on to become outstanding leaders. As referenced in the journals, the college was located at 188 Jessfield Road (now Wanhangdu Lu), which is on a bend in Suzhou Creek (formerally called Soochow Creek.) The campus was designed to incorporate both Chinese and Western architectural elements.

The university survived World War II, but when the Communists took over St. John's was broken up into several specialized schools such as the Shanghai Second Medical College, now the School of Medicine, and Shanghai Jiao Tong University. The campus itself is now the site of the East China University of Politics and Law.

In the late 19$^{th.}$ and early 20$^{th.}$ centuries there was a surge of piety and activism on many American college campuses which emphasized religion and social duty. James Mitchell was one of the thousands of students who responded to this calling between 1890 and 1920.

On graduation in 1915 from Trinity College in Hartford Connecticut, Arch applied to the Episcopal Board of Missions and was accepted to teach at St. John's College in Shanghai. His students, representing less than one tenth of one percent of the Chinese population, were on the Junior College level and could speak passable English. Their families would have needed an upper-class income to send them to St. John's, as the missionary institutions were more expensive than the few public colleges.

Classroom IIC Middle School, 1915

These students were taught typical western college subjects such as mathematics, banking, geometry, and, of course, English and Latin. The role of a mission school like St. John's was to encourage democratic and Christian beliefs. The students were already inclined to hold late nineteenth and early twentieth century liberal values and St. John's would have graduated socially conscious, free thinking, politically active young men, strongly committed to ending the Qing Dynasty and supporting a democratic Nationalist revolution. Later these same students would provide the type of leaders who supported the regime of Chiang Kai-shek, and some undoubtedly joined the Communist campaigns. (This information is from John Israel's book, *Student Nationalism in China – 1927-1937*, Stanford University Press, 1966.)

In 1881, the binding of upper-class girls' feet was a common practice, marriages were usually arranged, and girls had little or no access to formal education. In that year, the American Episcopal Church Mission founded St. Mary's Hall, a private school for girls. Other missionary-sponsored girls' schools sprung up at the same time, including the McTyeire School for Girls established by the American Southern Methodist Mission; nevertheless in 1909 there were still only 13,000 girls enrolled in school in all of China. One of the greatest impacts of the missionary movement was in training girls and thus raising the status of Chinese women.

When foreign residents had to depart from Shanghai in 1952, the McTyeire School was consolidated with St. Mary's and was renamed Number 3 Girls' School. Though today it is public rather than private, it remains one of Shanghai's most elite and highly-regarded schools with an active program of exchanges and interactions with American high schools and colleges.

Garden Party, St. Mary's Hall

Glossary

Anking   Anqing, a city on the Yangtze in southwestern Anhui province with a current population of over 5 million.

Canton   Guangzhou, located on the Pearl River, 75 miles northwest of Hong Kong, is the capital and most populous city of Guangdong Province. With over 13 million inhabitants is the third-largest city in China.

Chefoo   Yantai, situated on Bohai Gulf in Shandong Province, is its largest fishing village.

Chili Mountains Zhihli Mountains north of Beidaihe (Peitaiho) are referred to by JAM as the "Chili Mountains."

Chinkiang   Zhenjiang, a city in Jiagsu Province located on the southern bank of the Yangtze River near the Grand Canal.

Chung Wha Sheng Kung Wei A unity of American, British and Canadian Anglican missions founded in 1912 to create a single translation of the Book of Common Prayer. They had a mission compound in Yangchow.

coolie   An unskilled laborer often hired to transport goods or people. Formerly an indentured servant.

cumshaw   A tip or gratuity for services performed.

damascene JAM is referring here to damask, a highly-figured woven fabric.

Enoshima A Japanese island southwest of Yokohama, it has sandy beaches and is connected to the mainland with a modern causeway.

Fengtai A southwestern district of the city of Beijing.

Geiho Strait Kanmon Strait, the strait between Shimonoseki and Kitakyusu, Japan; it connects the Yellow and Inland seas.

Gulf of Chili Bohai Gulf, the body of water at the northeast end of the Yellow Sea. Tientsin and Peitaiho are both on the Bohai Gulf.

Hangyang One of the thirteen districts of the city of Wuhan

Hankow Hankou, one of three cities making up the municipality of Wuhan, the capital of Hubei Province. Today the metropolis contains more than 10 million people.

junk An ancient design of sailing ship in use for nearly two thousand years. There are many different types of junks.

Kiukiang Jiujiang, a city of about 5 million people on the southern shore of the Yangtze River in Jiangsu Province.

Kunshau Kunshan, a satellite city to Suzhou in the southeastern part of Jiangsu Province. It is the location of famous Tinglin Park and Ma'an Mountain.

Lares and Penates	A group of deities who protected the family and Roman state.
Mencius	Mengzi or "the philosopher Mang, sage of the second degree" was a Chinese philosopher, second only to Confucius, who lived in the third century, BC.
mirabile dictu	Latin for "wonderful to relate."
mofoo	A guide.
Nanking	Nanjing, city on the lower Yangtze River and capital of Jiangsu Province, it has a population of over 8 million. Nanjing has served as the capital city of many Chinese dynasties dating from the third century, BC.
Nankou Pass	Juyongguan Pass is the part of The Great Wall nearest to Bejing, being only about forty miles away. The Nankou area is now a suburb of that great city.
Nanyang	A city of 10 million people in the province of Henan. It is located about 600 miles west of Shanghai.
Pei-nyui-ting	Beiniuding Mountain, Qinghuangdao, Hebei Province. According to JAM, means "the mountain that backs the cow." It is a steep-sided hill with ladders leading to a temple on top.
Pei-tai-ho	Beidaihe, the name Pei-tai-ho is still used for the beach resort on the Bohai Gulf near this city. With a population of 66,000, Beidaihe is a district of the city of Qinhuangdao in Hebei Province.

168

Peking   Beijing, the capital of The People's Republic of China and its largest city with a population of over 20 million people.

Prukow   Pukou, on the opposite bank of the Yangtze River from Nanjing, is considered one of its districts. Where JAM took a ferry, there is now a bridge.

punka   A fan, often made of leaves, which is hung from the ceiling and operated by a servant.

Shantung   Shandong, coastal province in eastern China. Yentai (Cheefoo) is in Shandong province.

Soochow   Suzhou, located about 62 miles northwest of Shanghai, is one of the major tourist attractions in China. Settled 2,500 years ago, it now has a population of over 4 million. It is known for its stone bridges.

Tienstin   Tianjin, a metropolis of 15 million on the Bohai Gulf south of Beijing.

tiffin   A light noontime meal served in the English colonies. Often consisting of Indian curries, one can still enjoy this "meal" in the Tiffin Room at the Raffles Hotel in Singapore.

Toochin   This refers to the northern-most province of Vietnam during the French colonial period, also known as Tochin and Tonkin. The Toochin "boy" referred to in the journal would have been from this province.

topee   A lightweight hat or helmet made of plant pith covered with cloth; a pith helmet.

Tseng-Tse	Zengzi, or "Master Zeng", was a disciple of Confucius, who taught his grandson, who, in turn, taught Mang-Tse. He is known as one of the Four Sages of Confucianism.
Tsingtao	Qingdao, a major seaport and naval base on the Yellow Sea, is the home to more than 6 million people. The region was seized by Germany in 1898 and held until 1914.
Tszu-szu	Zisi, gransdon of Confucius and teacher of Mang Tse. He is credited with writing The Doctrine of the Mean, a guide to personal perfection through harmony and balance.
Tuchun	A Chinese military governor or warlord.
Van-Waung-Doo	The ferry landing next to St. John's University. It is located in the village of Zou Ka Doo where Jessfield Road intersects Suzhou Creek.
Weihaiwei	Weihai, a city on the Yellow Sea at the entrance to Bohai Gulf. It was leased to the British in 1898 to counter the Russian's leasing of Qingdao. It controls the seaward access to Beijing. It was returned to Chinese control in 1930.
Whangpoo River	Huangpu River, main river running through Shanghai. It is a tributary to the Yangtze and was created in the 4th century BC. Suzhou Creek runs into the Huangpoo.
Wuchang	A district of the metropolis of Wucan, is located on the southern bank of the Yangtze.
Wusih	Wuxi, city northwest of Suzhou on Taihu Lake.

Yangchow	Yangzhou, located on the north bank of the Yangtze River, is at the start of the Grand Canal.
Yen hui	Yan Hui, a contemporary and favorite disciple of Confucius.
yomen	Yoeman, a servant or retainer in a noble or royal household. In this case I believe it refers to an administrative assistant.
Zou Ka Doo	A small Chinese village surrounding St. John's University. The expanding city of Shanghai has swallowed up this native town along with the grave mounds and the surrounding countryside.

About the Editors:

John Hanson Mitchell is an American author with a list of ten books, five of which concentrate on a single square mile of land in eastern Massachusetts known as Scratch Flat. He has visited some of the sites mentioned in this book.

Hugh Powers Mitchell is a former social worker and an environmental activist. He was head of the New York Sierra Club and is a published poet. He also lectures on Warlord China.

CPSIA information can be obtained
at www.ICGtesting.com
Printed in the USA
FFOW02n0734190617
36838FF